A LONG
STRUGGLE

EDITED BY PAULINE WEBB

A LONG STRUGGLE

THE INVOLVEMENT OF THE WORLD COUNCIL OF CHURCHES IN
SOUTH AFRICA

WCC Publications, Geneva

Cover design: Edwin Hassink

ISBN 2-8254-1135-3

© 1994 WCC Publications, World Council of Churches,
150 route de Ferney, 1211 Geneva 2, Switzerland

Printed in Switzerland

Contents

About the Authors

Pauline Webb, a lay preacher, was organizer of religious broadcasting in the World Service of the BBC. She was vice-moderator of the WCC central committee from 1968 to 1975.

Baldwin Sjollema was the first director of the WCC's Programme to Combat Racism (PCR), from 1970 to 1981.

Elisabeth Adler was director of the Lay Academy of Berlin-Brandenburg, Berlin, and, after a six-month consultantship with PCR in 1973, a member of the PCR commission from 1975 to 1983.

Donna Katzin is director of South Africa Programs of the Interfaith Center for Corporate Responsibility in New York.

David Haslam is associate secretary for racial justice in the Churches Commission for Racial Justice, Council of Churches for Britain and Ireland, London, England.

Barney Pityana, who was director of the WCC's Programme to Combat Racism from 1988 to 1992, is now senior research officer at the Research Institute on Christianity in South Africa, University of Cape Town.

Charles Villa-Vicencio is professor of religion and society at the University of Cape Town, South Africa.

Philip Potter was general secretary of the World Council of Churches from 1972 to 1984.

Foreword

Few contemporary issues have more profoundly marked the life of the World Council of Churches and how people perceive it than the struggle against racism and in particular the involvement in South Africa. It was as a consequence of this struggle and its programmatic expression in the Programme to Combat Racism that a decisive shift in ecumenical perspective began to manifest itself. Instead of continuing to interpret world reality from the perspective of those responsible for maintaining "order", the ecumenical movement declared its solidarity with the victims of the structures of injustice and with their struggle for "liberation". The condemnation of racism as sin and the rejection of its theological justification as heresy were decisive in shaping ecumenical reflection about the unity of the church in its constitutive relationship to the quest for justice in human community.

For decades the apartheid system has been the focus of an intense struggle and of controversies surrounding the WCC's involvement in South Africa. Now that it is being transformed, it is possible and timely to retrace this long struggle. The Programme to Combat Racism, initiated in 1969, celebrates its 25th anniversary in 1994 at the moment when the whole people of South Africa have been able for the first time to elect their democratic representatives, marking the final point of the transition to a new order of society. The meeting of the WCC central committee in Johannesburg in January 1994 ushered in a new period of relationships between the worldwide Christian community and the people and the churches in South Africa.

This book, which reviews the history of WCC involvement in South Africa from different perspectives, has been written not to foster ecumenical triumphalism but to keep alive ecumenical memory. The lessons learned during "a long struggle" must not be forgotten on the way ahead, neither in South Africa nor in the ecumenical movement as a whole. The contributors as well as the editor have all been actively involved in shaping this chapter of ecumenical history. May their witness strengthen the ecumenical commitment to the promotion of justice and human rights wherever people are excluded because of race, sex, class or belief and denied their dignity as persons created in the image of God.

Konrad Raiser
General Secretary
World Council of Churches

Introduction

One of the consolations of growing older is that the time span grows shorter. The utopian dreams of youth can become impatient as the long years stretch dauntingly ahead and the struggle to turn vision into reality seems interminable. Then suddenly comes a turning point and time seems to collapse like a telescope. The distant horizon of hope becomes an immediate landscape, and the lone voices of prophecy become the popular wisdom of the day. It is time then for memories to stir and to record the journey thus far, so that the ultimate goal might be kept clear and the commitment to attaining it be as determined and persistent as ever.

The World Council of Churches and its Programme to Combat Racism has reached one such important turning point. The former will soon be celebrating its fiftieth birthday, the latter is marking its silver jubilee in 1994. Both began in prophetic zeal, inspired by the dreams of young and old, men and women, who saw a vision of unity which would break down the barriers that have for so many centuries hedged in the churches, divided the races and distorted the God-given design of human community. Like Joshua's army, they took up the trumpets to proclaim the truths of that kingdom in which all the walls would come tumbling down, only to discover how sturdy those barriers, buttressed by the prejudices of history, are. What seemed like an obvious act of obedience to God's word has become a long struggle, one that is as intense at the end of the twentieth century as it was at the beginning.

Yet that word of God has accomplished in our own time more than anyone dared to ask or expect. In extraordinary ways it has undermined even societies that claimed to be founded upon it. A visitor to South Africa cannot but be daunted by the sight of the great Voortrekker monument. It stands like a defiant bastion on the mountain opposite the parliament buildings in Pretoria. On a stone frieze is recorded the history of a people who firmly believed that God had called them to fight their way into a new nation where the native peoples would be subjugated and they themselves would inherit a promised land. That sense of divine vocation persisted into this century when the constitution of the Republic of South Africa was framed, beginning with these words of dedication:

> In humble submission to Almighty God, who controls the destiny of peoples and nations, who gathered our forebears together from many lands and gave them this their own; who has guided them from generation to generation; who has wondrously delivered them from the dangers that beset them...

It then went on to spell out the policy of segregation and discrimination known as apartheid, which denied the majority of the people inhabiting the land any share in its citizenship, many of their basic human rights and access to most of its wealth.

It is not surprising that a republic which thus claimed to be founded on the word of God should become particularly susceptible to the scrutiny of the international Christian community. It was not only a country blemished by the blasphemy of racism but one where churches flourished and where strong links had been forged with the military, financial and commercial power centres of the world. So from the earliest days of the ecumenical movement South Africa was a burden on the conscience of the world church and a challenge to its integrity.

Inevitably therefore, when the WCC launched its Programme to Combat Racism (PCR), South Africa became a major focus of its concern. Many of the WCC's member churches, whose own countries had strong alliances with South Africa, failed to recognize how deeply they themselves were implicated in the injustices being perpetrated there. So the long struggle began, not only in solidarity with those within South Africa who were working for the liberation of the oppressed, but also in confrontation with many outside South Africa who refused to acknowledge the ramifications of that oppression.

The story of that struggle is told in these pages. It is not particularly the story of heroes. There were many men and women whose personal witness and stance against apartheid deserves to be emblazoned in letters of gold. Among them were prophets and martyrs of our time, both within and beyond South Africa. Like Archbishop Trevor Huddleston, whose book about apartheid became a clarion call to a whole generation of Christians, they brought the churches *Naught for Your Comfort*. Many of them found their sphere of activity and protest beyond the structures of the church itself. They worked mainly in and through the Anti-Apartheid Movement, the International Defence and Aid Fund and a myriad of smaller action groups concentrating their attention upon aiding the oppressed peoples of South Africa in their liberation struggle.

Nor is this an account of the leaders who tower over the South African scene. Some of them have been both church leaders and political figures. In South Africa, possibly more than anywhere else in the world, public policy and religious faith have, for better and for worse, become inextricably intertwined. This has meant that, when the voices of the authentic leaders of the people were silenced in jail or by execution, it was incumbent upon church leaders to become the voice of the voiceless. And when the political leaders, like some modern Cyrus, became the unexpected instrument of God's purpose, those churches which had always supported the government had themselves to repent of their ways.

This book is rather a record of the attempts to mobilize churches across the world to make their witness heard against apartheid and in support of the struggle for justice for all God's children. In some ways it is a tedious story. Many of the fiercest battles were fought in church committee rooms where the only weapons were carefully worded resolutions. Others were tramped out in the streets where people stood in protest demonstrations or organized boycotts. Some took place in the awesome precincts of company board rooms where a few bold Davids confronted the Goliaths of the business and commercial worlds. Wherever the words of the prophets became events and the resolutions of the churches turned into actions, the debates became intense.

Significantly, much of the controversy concerned money, which proved to be more eloquent than any words. On the one hand, there was the argument about whether it was appropriate for the churches to use money symbolically through the Special Fund of the PCR to express solidarity with liberation movements which were turning in the last resort to armed struggle because they believed that to be the only way left to them to achieve their liberation. So, though it was constantly made clear that the Special Fund was itself an humanitarian and non-violent way of making their cause known, the question of the legitimacy of the use of force was regularly raised. On the other hand, there was even fiercer argument about the wisdom of withdrawing money invested in banks and companies which were fueling the military might of the apartheid regime. In this context there was little discussion about the legitimacy of armed force being used by the state to impose its policy of apartheid.

There was also surprisingly little theological debate, though PCR, like the World Council of Churches as a whole, based its actions on biblical convictions. Those convictions led to a general consensus — which finally in these latter years has been accepted even by the Dutch Reformed Church in South Africa itself — that any doctrine of apartheid is heresy and must be rejected in the light of God's word. That word of God is itself a two-edged sword, and those who brandish it can find it turning on them, dissecting their own anatomy. So recently the structure of the South African state has itself been undergoing radical surgery. There has been much pain and bloodshed, but there is also now a hope of healing and of the emergence of a whole, new nation. Trying to predict what will have happened even by the time this book is published is as precarious as making plans for a patient who has yet to recuperate from a long sickness. The support, the solidarity and the prayers of the Christian community will be needed in the struggle of the future as much as in the past.

In this book we record the history of that struggle so far. The first two chapters were written by Baldwin Sjollema, who was the first director of the Programme to Combat Racism. He shows how an ecumenical theology opposing racism was being formulated even in the days before the establishment of the World Council of Churches. That theology came to be expressed in the reports of the earliest assemblies. It reached a critical point, so far as relations with the South African churches were concerned, at the Cottesloe consultation of 1960. It continued to be drawn upon in subsequent resolutions addressing the South African situation in particular.

It was at the Uppsala assembly of 1968 that racism became a dominant theme on the ecumenical agenda, which led to the launching of PCR the following year. The second chapter shows how the debate initiated by this action-oriented programme affected the whole life of the WCC.

The following three chapters take up some of these issues as they affected regions of the world outside South Africa. Elisabeth Adler, who was the author of the first review of PCR, entitled *A Small Beginning* (1974), writes particularly from the background of her experience in what was then East Germany. In discussing the question of the churches and their political involvement, she emphasizes the importance of the theological debate around this issue, especially since in South Africa the state sought to justify the apartheid principle on theological grounds.

The important role of economic sanctions in undermining the apartheid system is highlighted in the chapter by Donna Katzin of the Interfaith Centre for Corporate Responsibility in the USA. She discusses how boycotts and campaigns against financial institutions that were buttressing the South African regime provoked vigorous debate about the effectiveness of such measures and the possible harm they might cause. She describes how US churches consulted with their partner churches in South Africa, so that information and economic strategies became internationalized.

David Haslam, director of the Office for Racial Justice of the Council of Churches in Britain and Ireland, takes up the story from the point of view of the churches in Europe. He emphasizes how the controversy surrounding the PCR became itself an effective means of education and awareness-building. Reluctant as the churches were to take any radical action, the programme led to the founding of many action groups in the UK, the Netherlands, Germany and Scandinavia, which became a spur to the institutional churches.

The book then turns to responses from within South Africa. Former PCR director Barney Pityana, of the Research Institute for Christianity in South Africa, undertakes a theological analysis of the reaction of South African churches, drawing out from it lessons on such matters as the relation between church and state, methods of doing theology and the need for a renewed understanding of the nature of the church.

Charles Villa-Vicencio of the Department of Religious Studies in the University of Cape Town goes to the nub of the debate about violence as it was understood by many churches at the height of the controversy surrounding the grants given to the liberation movements through the PCR Special Fund. Though they were specifically given for humanitarian work only, the question was raised as to how far this endorsed the armed struggle in which many of these movements were engaged. Claiming that the churches have always been ambivalent in their attitudes to the use of force, he goes on to discuss the different kinds of violence that have clouded the history of South Africa. He suggests that the nature of the violence still prevalent in South Africa has increased the urgency of finding non-violent ways of acting effectively in the cause of racial justice.

The last chapter on "The Task Ahead" is by Philip Potter, who has given a lifetime of service to the ecumenical movement and who, particularly as general secretary of the World Council of Churches from 1972-84, has been in the forefront of the struggle against racism. He assesses the continuing role of the ecumenical and international community in giving support to the churches in South Africa as they enable people to participate in the democratic process. He stresses the need for economic development which will benefit those whose lives have been the most impoverished through the effects of apartheid. He calls the churches of the world to that repentance which is the prerequisite of reconciliation, and to that sharing of resources which enables all women and men to enjoy the full and abundant life which is their rightful heritage.

The authors and editor of this book are indebted to many people who, in the midst of busy agendas, have given what help they could in researching old records, compiling material and preparing manuscripts for publication. Special thanks are due to Brigitte Berthouzoz, who acted as research assistant to Baldwin Sjollema, and Simphiwe Javu, research assistant to Barney Pityana. We also acknowledge the help given by Deborah Robinson and Mary Balikungeri, executive secretary and administrative assistant in the present PCR team, now part of the WCC's Programme Unit on Justice, Peace and Creation. The Office of Communication has finally seen the book through the press. We are grateful also for financial help received from our sponsors: Norwegian Church Aid, the Church of Sweden Mission and Interchurch Aid of the Netherlands Reformed Church.

The book is dedicated to all those both in South Africa and beyond who have engaged in the struggle, in some cases with great heroism and at sacrificial cost, and in others with the foot-slogging persistence of those who have pursued the path of justice without growing weary. They have borne their share of ignominy for the sake of Christ and of their oppressed brothers and sisters. They have been sustained as they have drawn constantly on the resources of a spirituality needed for this kind of prolonged struggle. Among such resources, while I have been preparing this manuscript, I have found help from a book of daily readings published by Pax Christi entitled *Peacemaking Day by Day*. It so happens that on the day when I am writing this introduction, the quotation comes from the pen of a prophet of our time who took a vow of silence as a Trappist monk but shared the struggle of the oppressed through his writings and his prayers. Thomas Merton writes, "Christ our Lord did not come to bring peace to the world as a kind of spiritual tranquillizer. He brought to his disciples a vocation and a task — to struggle in the world of violence to establish his peace not only in their own hearts but in society itself."

That struggle continues, and calls for our continued solidarity in word, deed and prayer: *Nkosi Sikelel'iAfrika*.

God bless Africa — and give her peace.

Pauline Webb

1

The Initial Challenge

BALDWIN SJOLLEMA

Ecumenical theology denouncing racism was not invented by the World Council of Churches. Long before the WCC came into existence, leaders in the Student Christian Movement (SCM) and the International Missionary Council (IMC) had made theological affirmations against racism. As early as 1921, J.H. Oldham was asked by the IMC to study and write about what was then called "the race problem". With prophetic impatience he said:

> Christianity is not primarily a philosophy but a crusade. As Christ was sent by the Father, so he sends his disciples to set up in the world the kingdom of God. His coming was a declaration of war — a war to the death against the powers of darkness. He was manifested to destroy the works of the devil. Hence when Christians find in the world a state of things that is not in accord with the truth which they have learned from Christ, their concern is not that it should be explained but that it should be ended. In that temper we must approach everything in the relations between races that cannot be reconciled with the Christian ideal. [1]

At its conference in Jerusalem in 1928 the IMC declared:

> Any discrimination against human beings on the ground of race or colour, any selfish exploitation and any oppression of man by man is a denial of the teaching of Jesus. [2]

And in 1937 the Oxford world conference on Life and Work added:

> The assumption by any race or nation of supreme blood or destiny must be emphatically denied by Christians as without foundation in fact and wholly alien to the heart of the gospel. [3]

These statements from the early years of the ecumenical movement were strong for their time. But there was little or no active follow-up. Though the WCC, in process of formation after 1938 but not yet officially established, was involved in rescuing Jews from the Nazis, it was only after the second world war that the issue of racism was forced on the churches with new vigour. The WCC was established in 1948 — the same year as the National Party came to power in South Africa and the state of Israel was established, both of which events had profound consequences for the life and witness of the WCC.

In 1950 the law constituting the foundation of apartheid was enacted. The cornerstone of the apartheid edifice was laid. Christians the world over began to realize that a stronger international response was needed. The WCC, through its Commission of the Churches on International Affairs (CCIA), expressed its concern to the South African member churches and offered to send a multi-racial ecumenical delegation to visit them. But the South African member churches reacted negatively, saying that sending such a delegation would cause problems, although they were ready to receive a WCC representative. In 1952 the WCC's first general secretary, W.A. Visser 't Hooft, visited South Africa himself to establish closer contacts between the Council and the churches. While raising pertinent questions with them about the role of the churches in an apartheid society, he suggested at that time that the word apartheid had several meanings, including "separate development of the races so that each may have the fullest opportunity for growth".[4] This view was shared by other church leaders in the West. More significant, however, was the role Visser 't Hooft's visit played in preparing for a debate on the race issue at the WCC Evanston assembly in 1954. This debate resulted in a general declaration that "any form of segregation based on race, colour or ethnic origin is contrary to the gospel and is incompatible with the Christian doctrine of man and with the nature of the church of Christ".[5] Following Evanston, the WCC created a Secretariat of Racial and Ethnic Relations.

Six years later, the shots that rang out from Sharpeville, where police fired indiscriminately on crowds protesting against the pass laws, shocked the world into realizing how repressive the apartheid regime was. As a result of the Sharpeville massacre, black resistance hardened. The political movements — the African National Congress (ANC) and the Pan Africanist Congress (PAC) — were banned and several of their leaders forced into exile. For the two movements, it was the beginning of a thirty-year period of intensive liberation struggle led from outside the country. The ANC felt compelled to change its half-century-old non-violent opposition to the white regime into an armed struggle. Internationally, a new era dawned for the anti-apartheid movement. At the request of the United Nations Security Council, the secretary general took a strong and resolute line against Prime Minister Hendrik Verwoerd, architect of the apartheid legislation. But after meeting with him Dag Hammarskjöld had to conclude: "This is going to be far harder than I thought. He [Verwoerd] really believes that the Bible has made his Whites superior to the Blacks."[6]

Within South Africa, the Sharpeville massacre caused sharp conflict between the Nederduitse Gereformeerde Kerk (Dutch Reformed Church) and the English-speaking churches. The DRC, whose branches in the Transvaal and the Cape were members of the WCC, acknowledged shortcomings on the part of the church and the government, but they continued to support "independent, distinctive development" provided it was "carried out in a just and honourable way". To this, Anglican Archbishop Joost de Blank reacted sharply, stating that black protest was directed not only at the government but also at the churches which supported its apartheid policies. He asked the WCC to expel the DRC from its membership.

The Cottesloe consultation

It was in this context that the WCC, after sending its associate general secretary, Robert Bilheimer, to South Africa three times for intensive discussions, took a new initiative. It convened an historic multi-racial consultation of its eight member churches in South Africa together with WCC representatives at Cottesloe in December 1960. The meeting was aimed at establishing the facts of the situation in South Africa and outlining the "Christian attitude towards race relations". The Anglicans threatened to withdraw from the planned consultation when outspoken Anglican Bishop Ambrose Reeves, who had been nominated as a delegate, was deported; but in the end, the meeting went ahead without the government's allowing him to attend. Eighty South African church delegates (a quarter of whom were black), one observer from the Christian Council and six representatives of the WCC met for a week on the basis of prepared memoranda by each church. For many of the South African delegates, it was their first time living with people of other races. Black delegates spoke of the pain and suffering apartheid caused their people.

A statement finally approved by the required eighty percent rejected all forms of racial discrimination, but admitted that

> widely divergent convictions have been expressed on the basic issues of apartheid. They range on the one hand from the judgement that it is unacceptable in principle, contrary to the Christian calling and unworkable in practice, to the conviction on the other hand that a policy of differentiation can be defended from the Christian point of view, that it provides the only realistic solution to the problems of race relations and is therefore in the best interests of the various population groups.[7]

The Cottesloe statement also said that all racial groups had an equal right to make their contribution towards the life of the country. It declared that no one should be excluded from any church on the grounds of race, and urged that spiritual unity must find expression in acts of common worship, witness and fellowship. It spoke of the disintegrating effects of migrant labour, of wages well below the minimum standard and of the right to own land, wherever one was domiciled. It stated that there is no scriptural ground to prohibit mixed marriages, but added that the well-being of the community and pastoral responsibility require giving due consideration to certain factors which might make such marriages inadvisable.

The Cottesloe consultation became of crucial importance for the future of church-state relations in South Africa. Prime Minister Verwoerd and the Afrikaner Broederbond — the secret Brotherhood of Afrikaners, to which all government ministers belonged and which effectively ran the country — were furious. Declaring that the meeting had been an attempt to interfere with South African internal affairs, they urged the churches not only to reject its outcome, but also to leave the WCC and support the policies of the National Party. Delegates of a smaller Afrikaner member church, the Hervormde Kerk, distanced themselves from the consultation, stating that "separate development is the only just solution of our racial problems". They placed on record "our gratefulness to the government for all the positive steps it had already taken to solve the problem..." By April 1961 both the Hervormde Kerk and the much bigger and more influential DRC had left the WCC.

The WCC's role throughout the Cottesloe meeting had been to try to draw the member churches out of isolation and to foster ecumenical fellowship. But no less important was the need for the Council to witness to the strong convictions about racial justice laid down by the Evanston assembly. Cottesloe laid bare a deep conflict between the demand for justice and the concern for unity. Ought the Council to risk a break in the ecumenical fellowship because of the demand for justice now? During and after Cottesloe this question was openly asked and covertly feared. The problem of race relations in South Africa coloured all else. And the churches were very much part of that problem.

A year later, the WCC New Delhi assembly (1961) sent a message to Christians in South Africa, expressing regret over the departure of the three Afrikaner churches but reminding them that Christians the world over were involved in the struggle to eliminate segregation. The message added: "We know that in the name of Christ, many in South Africa are engaged in this struggle." Addressed to South African Christians, and not just churches, the message expressed solidarity with all those who felt isolated in their witness after their churches had opposed the results of Cottesloe. The assembly reinforced the basic position already taken at Evanston (1954) by stating:

> The struggle between the old privileged groups and the new aspiring ones is intensified and extended... The church is called to strive actively for racial justice. Christians should not be tied to any one way of action but should make creative use of various means — conciliation, litigation, legislation, mediation, protest, economic sanctions and non-violent action — including cooperation with secular groups working towards the same ends... The churches should identify themselves with the oppressed race... Racism... often causes oppressed people to resort to violence when they have no other option... All races, as indeed all persons, have their own unique contribution to make to the fellowship of human society but we cannot agree that this is a reason for "separate development"... The expression "separate but equal" is in concrete actuality a contradiction in terms. [8]

The mandate of the WCC Secretariat on Racial and Ethnic Relations was strengthened. It came under the fine leadership of the Japanese-American theologian Daisuke Kitagawa, who had a particular gift of being able to listen and so to gain the confidence of the groups involved in racial conflict.

In South Africa, many of the Cottesloe delegates became discouraged. They felt isolated by the decision of their churches to break with the ecumenical fellowship. The WCC encouraged them to set up ecumenical study groups to maintain regular communication among themselves. In 1962, a small group of ministers and lay persons launched an independent ecumenical monthly journal *Pro Veritate*. It demolished the biblical justification of apartheid and called for cooperation between churches and Christians in a united witness. C.F. Beyers Naudé, a former moderator of the DRC of Transvaal, who had played an important part in the Cottesloe meeting, became its editor. Together with Fred van Wyk he was the main instigator of the Christian Institute of Southern Africa, the most daring attempt among white anti-apartheid ministers — from both English-speaking and Afrikaner churches — to speak up about the violation of the gospel by the churches. The Institute courageously provided the vision and dynamic for a relatively small but growing movement among Christians who sought to give a practical witness to their Christian faith. It organized discussion groups across the country, maintained an ecumenical library and disseminated vital information on apartheid and its consequences. Most importantly, it responded to the plea for assistance from approximately 2400 African independent churches, which represented about 20 percent of the total African population, in the formation of the African Independent Churches' Association (AICA) with over 250 member bodies.

A widening concern

In 1963, the WCC's central committee, meeting in Rochester (USA), urged white Christians in South Africa to repudiate by deeds and words "all that weakens their witness to Christ". Christians outside were asked to inform the rest of the world about what was happening. At the same time the WCC supported a number of projects, including ecumenical conference centres (Wilgespruit and Forest Sanctuary), and continued to provide scholarships for South African students at the Ecumenical Institute of Bossey and elsewhere.

This was largely due to the work of Z.K. Matthews, a lawyer who was a delegate at the Cottesloe consultation and joined the WCC staff in 1962 as the first Africa secretary of its Division of Inter-Church Aid, Refugee and World Service. His presence in the WCC and his frequent visits to Africa and contacts with member churches and the UN were of particular importance in sharpening the WCC's understanding of the African people's struggle for liberation. He had been a professor at Fort Hare and later its acting principal before becoming chairman of the African National Congress. This led to his arrest in 1956 on a charge of high treason, for which he was tried and acquitted. In 1964 Matthews visited Lesotho, South Africa and Southern Rhodesia on behalf of the WCC to assess the problems relating to victims of the policy of apartheid. In a confidential report he gave evidence of imprisonment, charges, sentences and detention without trial. Over half of those defended in the courts, he said, were found not guilty and discharged. Explaining the urgency of legal defence, he urged that ecumenical funds be made available for it. He also discussed the need for a refugee reception centre for South Africans in Lusaka.[9]

As the situation in southern Africa deteriorated, it became clear that new initiatives by the WCC were needed. The race problem was provoking increasing anger and violence. There was growing resentment about the treatment of the black peoples and an increasing demand for action. In 1964, the WCC's Department on Church and Society, in cooperation with the All Africa Conference of Churches (AACC), the Mindolo Ecumenical Foundation and the South African Institute for Race Relations convened a consultation at Kitwe, Zambia, which brought together individuals from various parts of southern Africa, who spoke out as a group of Christians. There was a strong delegation from South Africa, most of whom had staunchly defended the Cottesloe findings. The purpose of the meeting was to ask what Christians could and ought to do. There was careful scrutiny of the political, economic, social and ecclesiastical facts and their interpretation.

The consultation was chaired by Daisuke Kitagawa; and Z.K. Matthews gave one of the most impressive speeches, tracing the long history of negotiation between black organizations and white governments in South Africa and their failure to achieve any real progress. Until its banning in 1960, Matthews noted, the ANC had rejected violence, but now blacks in South Africa despaired of achieving political change by peaceful means. Though Matthews did not advocate violence, he clearly indicated that for many of his people violence was now unavoidable. The question is "not whether the latter methods will succeed, but whether they begin to appear to the African in South Africa as the only methods open to him". He also criticized the attitude of the Western powers, which had shown little sympathy for the Africans' struggle.

Another committed Christian participant at the Mindolo consultation was Eduardo Mondlane, the leader of Frelimo, the liberation movement in Mozambique. Mondlane had been a youth participant at the Evanston assembly and had been much impressed by the debates among the young people there. He had studied in the USA, taught at Syracuse University and held a prominent UN staff position before deciding to give his full energy to the liberation of his people. Mondlane explained how in his country Frelimo had had to decide to involve itself in violent resistance against the Portuguese colonial rulers, but said he had come to the Mindolo consultation not only to explain his position but also to discuss the moral and spiritual problems with which he and his organization were now confronted.

Visser 't Hooft reminded participants of the views held by John Calvin and John Knox, who had taken the position that in certain situations of oppression one of the "good works" of Christians could be to eliminate the tyrant. Such resistance had also been seen as necessary by some Christians — notably Dietrich Bonhoeffer — in Germany during the Nazi period. Though warning against the dangers of violence, Visser 't Hooft agreed that armed resistance could not be entirely ruled out.

The Mindolo meeting thus reflected a new reality. The conflict had deepened since Cottesloe. The warnings were clear: peaceful solutions were becoming more and more difficult.

The report and recommendations from Mindolo accepted the need for internal action in South Africa, including boycotts, general strikes and, as a last resort, planned industrial disruption, to secure a change of government policy. The church had to recognize that individual Christians were becoming involved in economic strife and should not shrink from its pastoral responsibility to them. It should also continue to press for the removal of restrictions on freedom of association and of collective bargaining by the black population. Africans, the meeting claimed, should have the right to freehold tenure and more equitable distribution of land.

The participants felt that the world community should not only criticize and condemn the unacceptable policy of the South African government, but also be prepared to produce constructive alternative solutions. On the issue of violence, they said: "Many African leaders maintain that violence has never been desired or sought if any other mode of effective negotiation could be established or remained open. The consultation feared that if the urgency of the situation is not recognized, negotiation established and further effective measures taken, violence will increase."[10]

Meanwhile, the race issue was moving higher on the agendas of many ecumenical meetings. Not only in southern Africa, but also in the USA and Britain, the churches were confronted with serious situations of racial violence and hatred. In the USA, Martin Luther King Jr and the civil rights movement were letting the nation know that its black population was no longer willing to suffer silently and wait patiently for basic human rights. Hundreds of US cities were engulfed in civil turmoil, with violence trembling just below the surface.

At the important WCC world conference on Church and Society in Geneva in 1966, the issue of racism was dramatically highlighted by the refusal of the South African government to issue a passport to Anglican bishop Alphaeus Zulu, one of the presidents of the conference. Martin Luther King, also compelled by racial conflict to stay in Chicago, had to cancel his engagement to preach in the Geneva cathedral, and his taped sermon was broadcast from an empty pulpit.

Many of the contemporary situations reviewed by the Geneva conference demonstrated the growing menace of racism across the world. The International Court of Justice had decided, by a single vote on technical grounds, to throw out a six-year suit by Ethiopia and Liberia to end South Africa's control of Namibia, thereby leaving unchanged the apartheid administration over the territory. There was growing impatience with the inability of the British government to make any progress in finding a solution to the problem of Rhodesia, where a white government had unilaterally declared independence. Ill-feeling between the races was being intensified by the Vietnam war where Americans were fighting Asians.

The conference underlined the need for the churches to see racial and ethnic problems in the context of the political and economic structures of society. It recognized that countries with socialist, capitalist and mixed economies all presented different contexts within which to view ethnic and racial problems, but "basic human rights as seen from a Christian perspective must not be compromised under any circumstances in any manner. Otherwise, Christian faith fails to provide that unity of mankind which transcends political and economic factors".[11]

The demand for action

By the time of the 1968 WCC assembly in Uppsala, Sweden, the race issue had taken on new dimensions and increased in intensity all around the world.

The assembly began with a commemoration of the assassinated Martin Luther King, who was to have been the preacher at the opening worship in the Uppsala cathedral. The silencing of his prophetic voice had stunned the world.

The Vietnam and Biafra wars, both raging at the time of the assembly, had clear racial and ethnic overtones. Liberation wars against Portuguese colonialism were intensifying in Guinea-Bissau, Angola and Mozambique. In South Africa itself Umkhonto we Sizwe — the ANC's armed wing — had been established. The year 1968 was also a time of unprecedented student confrontation in the USA, France and Germany. In the USA, armed black people had occupied churches and church offices.

At the assembly, there was a growing recognition by many delegates that racism was a major issue in their own countries. Many reported local and national racial tensions and advocated a strong and leading role for the WCC in the struggle for justice and reconciliation. Small groups of concerned participants — both delegates and staff — met daily throughout the assembly to discuss concrete proposals for action. Two speakers at the assembly further influenced the deliberations. One was the African-American writer James Baldwin, son of a Baptist minister. In a vibrant speech on the theme "White Racism or World Community", he introduced himself as "one of God's creatures whom the Christian church has most betrayed". Recapitulating the long story of racial injustice, he charged that "long ago, for a complex of reasons, but among them power, the Christian personality split into two — into dark and light, and is now bewildered and at war with itself... I wonder if there is left in the Christian civilizations the moral energy, the spiritual daring to atone, to repent, to be born again?"[12]

Baldwin's passionate speech was followed by the more measured oratory of the permanent representative of the UK at the UN, Lord Caradon. He analyzed how the worsening relationships between the races were now inextricably woven into the problems of poverty and suggested an international campaign under the courageous leadership of the WCC. Calls were also made to link the elimination of racism to a redistribution of power.

The cry for action was heard, though for many church leaders it was difficult to digest. The assembly decided that the WCC should "undertake a crash programme to guide the Council and member churches in the urgent matter of racism". [13] While leaving the details of such a programme to the central committee, the assembly stated clearly that "the racial crisis... is to be taken as seriously as the threat of nuclear war. The revolt against racism is one of the most inflammatory elements of the social revolution now sweeping the earth; it is fought at the level of mankind's deepest and most vulnerable emotions — the universal passion for human dignity. We submit that this crisis will grow worse unless we understand the historical phenomenon of white racism." [14]

The assembly placed particular emphasis on white racism, "which has special historical significance because its roots lie in powerful, highly developed countries", defining it as the "conscious or unconscious belief in the inherent superiority of persons of European ancestry... coupled with the belief in the innate inferiority of all darker peoples, especially those of African ancestry...". [15] Similarly, it spoke out strongly on the economic and political aspects of racism:

> Racism is linked with economic and political exploitation. The churches must be actively concerned for the economic and political well-being of exploited groups so that their statements and actions may be relevant. In order that victims of racism may regain a sense of their own worth and be enabled to determine their own future, the churches must make economic and educational resources available to underprivileged groups for their development to full participation in the social and economic life of their communities. They should also withdraw investments from institutions that perpetuate racism... The churches must also work for the change of those political processes which prevent the victims of racism from participating fully in the civic and governmental structures of their countries... The churches must eradicate all forms of racism from their own life. That many have not done so, particularly where institutional racism assumes subtle forms, is a scandal. [16]

This was the cornerstone Uppsala laid, on which the WCC's future involvement in combating racism was built. The delegates decided to move from words to action and from giving charitable aid to victims of racial hatred to strengthening groups of the racially oppressed people themselves. Similarly, they felt that priority should go to eliminating institutional racism rather than concentrating on improving individual race relations.

This change in emphasis would have far-reaching consequences for the WCC's relations with South Africa. The situation in that country had raised a number of theological issues: the meaning of saying that Christ is on the side of the oppressed, the nature of the church in terms of its oneness and diversity, its solidarity with the oppressed and its reconciling task, structural violence in the context of church-state relationships.

The shift in the WCC's position at Uppsala was in no small measure due to the changed composition of the Council's constituency. The WCC was becoming more truly a world council. In 1948, 42 of the 147 churches which formed the Council were from third-world countries (including 10 from African churches in South Africa, Egypt and Ethiopia). Twenty years later, by the time of the fourth assembly, their number had increased to 103 out of 253. Of the 41 African churches, the majority were now from independent Africa. The suffering and active involvement in the struggle of countless Christians, particularly in southern Africa and the US, was having its impact. The presumed assassination of Albert Luthuli and the condemnation to life imprisonment of Nelson Mandela — and of many more whose names never reached the headlines — had a strong impact on the life of the ecumenical movement. The victims of racism and colonialism had made their own analysis of the situation and their demand was unambiguously stated. They wanted action from the WCC itself.

NOTES

[1] J.H. Oldham, *Christianity and the Race Problem*, London, SCM, 1926, p.26.
[2] *The Jerusalem Meeting of the IMC*, Vol. IV, *The Christian Mission in the Light of Race Conflict*, New York, International Missionary Council, 1928, p.195.
[3] *The Churches Survey Their Task,* report of the 1937 Oxford conference on Church, Community and State, London, Allen & Unwin, 1937, p.231.
[4] W.A. Visser 't Hooft, "Visit to the South African Churches: Report to the Central Committee of the WCC, 1952", *The Ecumenical Review*, V, no. 2, January 1953, p.181.
[5] *The Evanston Report*, London, SCM, 1955, p.158.
[6] Quoted by George Ivan Smith, *The Guardian* (London), 14 April 1993.
[7] *Cottesloe Consultation: The Report*, Johannesburg, 1961, p.73; also published in *The Ecumenical Review*, XIII, no. 2, January 1961, pp.1ff.
[8] *The New Delhi Report*, ed. W.A. Visser 't Hooft, London, SCM, 1962, pp.102-105; cf. p.324.
[9] Monica Wilson, *Freedom for My People*, London, Rex Collings, 1981, p.208.
[10] *Christians and Race Relations in Southern Africa*. Report on an Ecumenical Consultation, Kitwe, Geneva, WCC, 1964, p.13.
[11] *Christians in the Technical and Social Revolutions of Our Time*, report of the 1966 Geneva world conference on Church and Society, Geneva, WCC, 1967, p.161.
[12] *The Uppsala Report 1968*, ed. N. Goodall, Geneva, WCC, 1968, p.130.
[13] *Ibid.*, p.242.
[14] *Ibid.*, p.241.
[15] *Ibid.*
[16] *Ibid.*, p.66.

2

Eloquent Action

BALDWIN SJOLLEMA

The turning point in the WCC's opposition to racism came when the challenging words were translated into eloquent action. This happened as the result of the consultation held in Notting Hill, London, in 1969, convened by the WCC under the leadership of its second general secretary, Eugene Carson Blake. Its task was to explore the nature, causes and consequences of racism worldwide and to make recommendations to the WCC about its own future involvement and that of its member churches. The WCC executive committee had instructed that the consultation focus attention on "the problems of white racism", not excluding "the consideration of various expressions of counter-racism or other forms of racism". White racism in southern Africa, the USA and Europe was thus the main issue at the Notting Hill consultation.

At Notting Hill, leaders from the ecumenical movement and representatives of radical movements struggling for racial justice and liberation confronted one another for the first time in an international context. The keynote address at the consultation was to have been delivered by Eduardo Mondlane, but three days after he had accepted the invitation, he was assassinated by a parcel bomb. The death of this committed Christian and dynamic leader was a serious blow to Frelimo and to the people of Mozambique; the loss was also deeply felt by the WCC, to which he had contributed much. Mondlane's place as a speaker at the consultation was taken by Oliver Tambo, chairman of the ANC and an active Anglican layman. Addressing a public meeting in Church House, Westminster, he was frequently interrupted by strident hecklers from the National Front who had invaded the gallery and howled down abuse on him. Tambo spoke forcefully of "a worldwide revolution involving the great majority of peoples of the world, aimed at replacing the old order of human society with a new order, founded on a proper understanding of the nature of man, the meaning of justice and the course of human history". Both he and Archbishop Trevor Huddleston spoke of the Western concept of

"Christian civilization" as a subtle and ingenious device to foster acceptance of the doctrine of white superiority and black inferiority.

Tambo quoted words President Kenneth Kaunda of Zambia had spoken at the UN: "We are determined to avoid violence where this is possible but we cannot and will not do this at the expense of the tremendous suffering, oppression and exploitation of the majority in southern Africa."[1] And Huddleston ended with a quotation from Alan Paton, putting these words into the mouth of an old African priest: "I have one great fear in my heart, that when they [the whites] are turned to loving, we shall be turned to hating."[2]

A statement adopted by the consultation included the notable recommendation that "all else failing, the church and churches support resistance movements, including revolutions, which are aimed at the elimination of political or economic tyranny which makes racism possible".

Three months later, the WCC executive and central committees, meeting in Canterbury, were presented with the report of the Notting Hill consultation, including the recommendations for a WCC Programme to Combat Racism. Blake introduced the debate in Canterbury by saying:

> Since 1954, the WCC has generally spoken well and acted dynamically on race and racism. But the fact is that Christians have not either deracisized their own structures and life nor have they made a very significant contribution to the improvement of race relations in the nations and in the world. We must ask why we have so far failed. We must examine the implications of the general coincidence of whiteness with economic, political and military power. We must decide whether a new programme of study and action, with the emphasis on action, should be undertaken.[3]

The outline of the initial five-year programme foresaw a range of strategies: teams of enquiry, consultations on selected issues, opportunities for confrontation between those holding different positions on the meaning of racial justice and the methods for attaining it, assisting member churches in developing strategies for combating racial injustice, collecting and circulating the best analyses of racism, encouraging member churches and national and regional councils of churches to make racism a priority concern in their own programmes. The WCC itself was to develop programme projects and set up a Special Fund to Combat Racism.

Discussions centred on this last recommendation. The Special Fund was largely based on the need to symbolize a redistribution of power. This concept had replaced the suggestion of "reparation", which had dominated much of the debate at Notting Hill. One of the criteria of the Fund stipulated that it was "to support organizations that combat racism, rather than the welfare organizations that alleviate the effects of racism".

Its main purpose was to strengthen the organizational capability of racially oppressed groups. Grants would be given for humanitarian purposes, after careful consideration by the executive committee, but without control of the specific manner in which they were spent; and southern Africa would have priority in view of the gravity of the racial conflict in that area.

After a lengthy and heated debate, the central committee adopted an "Ecumenical Programme to Combat Racism" (PCR), outlining the main scope and focus of its mandate:

- Racism is not an unalterable feature of human life. Like slavery... it can and must be eliminated. In the light of the gospel and in accordance with its principles and methods, Christians must be involved in this struggle and, wherever possible, in association with all people of goodwill... The fight against racism in all its forms must be set in the context of the struggle for world community.
- Racism is not confined to certain countries or continents. It is a world problem. White racism is not its only form... It is the coincidence, however, of an accumulation of wealth and power in the hands of the white peoples... which is the reason for a focus on the various forms of *white* racism in different parts of the world.
- In our ecumenical fellowship there are churches from all parts of the world, some of which have benefitted and some of which have suffered from racially exploitative economic systems. What is needed is an ecumenical act of solidarity which would help to stem the deterioration in race relations. To do this our action must cost something and must be affirmative, visible and capable of emulation.
- The churches must move beyond charity grants and traditional programming to relevant and sacrificial action leading to new relationships of dignity and justice among all men and become agents for the radical reconstruction of society. There can be no justice in our world without a transfer of economic resources to undergird the redistribution of political power and to make cultural self-determination meaningful. In this transfer of resources a corporate act by the ecumenical fellowship of churches can provide a significant moral lead. [4]

The central committee, after some hesitation because of the principle involved and despite the Council's weak financial situation, decided to make US$200,000 available to the Fund out of its own reserves.

Since white racism was to be the main focus of the PCR's attention, it was clear that southern and South Africa would become one of the main areas of concern. South Africa was not the only example of the connection between white racism and economic and military power, nor was it the only case of racism by a minority over a majority. The South African government, however, had made itself special by claiming to defend "Western Christian civilization". The way in which it made this claim was a challenge to Christian faith and theology, to the church and to the fellowship of churches.

Immediate reactions to the PCR

Following the central committee's acceptance of the Notting Hill recommendations, an international advisory committee went immediately to work drafting the criteria for the Fund and recommending the first grants to the WCC executive committee meeting at Arnoldshain, Germany, in September 1970. These were approved. Among the organizations receiving grants were several liberation movements in southern Africa.

After the meeting, a short press release was distributed to journalists. Before the WCC had time to brief the churches likely to be most affected, South African Prime Minister John Vorster seized the opportunity and spoke out vehemently in parliament. He accused the WCC of being communist-infiltrated and providing terrorist organizations with funds for buying arms. The charge that the WCC had committed itself to "support terrorism" was headlined in many newspapers both in and beyond South Africa. The South African minister of foreign affairs spoke of the WCC support for organizations "whose actions consist of crimes of violence like murder, arson, armed robbery and others which are aimed at all sections of the civilian population, including innocent women and children".

Never had any action by the WCC received so much attention both in and outside the churches. At the same time the liberation movements, which until then had hardly appeared on the map of Christian concerns, were brought to the attention of the wider church public.

The PCR quickly became identified with southern Africa and was seen by some as a kind of church anti-apartheid movement. Programmes and projects with oppressed racial groups in Australia, New Zealand and North and South America, relating mainly to land rights, were hardly mentioned by its critics. The debate concentrated almost exclusively on support to "illegal" southern African liberation movements outlawed by the state and the churches' so-called involvement in violence. Uppermost in the minds of many Western politicians and strategists was the fact that South Africa played a key role as part of the southern flank of NATO. Any weakening of that role was to be countered, they said. Articles appeared on the vulnerability of the Cape Route and the need to protect the transport of oil and other minerals.[5]

The grants were also condemned by most churches in South Africa. They criticized the WCC for its support of "liberation movements" committed to a violent overthrow of the South African regime. But the South African Council of Churches (SACC), in a public statement, made it clear that despite the prime minister's warning against maintaining ties with the WCC, all the churches affiliated with the SACC had decided to retain their membership. The SACC criticized the WCC, complaining that the churches had not been informed beforehand about the action to be taken, but also condemned racism in South Africa and called for positive action to bring about reconciliation and racial justice.

The member churches in South Africa asked for a consultation with the WCC. In 1971, Blake agreed to such a consultation, requesting visas for a delegation of 18 persons representing the central committee and WCC staff to go to South Africa. Vorster, however, made the meeting impossible by laying down three conditions: first, the delegation would have to stay at Jan Smuts airport in Johannesburg — it could not visit the country and the churches; second, the only subject for discussion could be the WCC grants to "terrorist" organizations for the buying of arms; and third, the WCC delegation should be considerably reduced in size. Saying that the WCC could not agree to these terms for the visit, Blake indicated that the consultation would have to be indefinitely postponed.

The WCC was receiving a good deal of support as well, notably in messages from the AACC and from President Kaunda of Zambia, but as importantly through informal signs of support from black people in South Africa itself, both inside and outside the churches. Invariably, however, they did not want to be quoted for fear of reprisals.

One of the first open pleas for understanding of the WCC's action came from Beyers Naudé, the director of the Christian Institute. In *Pro Veritate*, he called attention to the

> silence of more than 18 million voices of the black population of South Africa... They dare not express what they really feel... For millions of our non-white population all the loud protests and condemnations of the decision of the World Council sounded hollow and empty because they had so little of the necessary self-condemnation, of a protest against a racial system and a policy with all its injustice which the whites are stubbornly maintaining. The more violent the reaction on the part of the whites, the more convinced did the non-whites become that their salvation from the slavery of apartheid will not come from the white Pharaohs but that they can only expect it from a Moses from their own ranks who at some time ("God alone knows when", as one of them put it) would speak the liberating word and perform the liberating deed. Talking is no longer enough. The time for pious words is past.[6]

Other messages of support came from organizations advocating non-violence like the International Fellowship of Reconciliation and the Southern Christian Leadership Conference in the USA.

The abortive proposal for the 1971 visit to South Africa showed the problem of communication between the WCC and its member churches there. Continuous misunderstandings arose on both sides because of a lack of information and interpretation, which resulted in sometimes angry reactions and exchanges of correspondence. Although the Vorster government did not succeed in making any of the churches leave the WCC, relationships were strained. Blake and particularly Philip Potter, who succeeded him as WCC general secretary in 1972, tried to remedy the situation by allowing additional guests representing South African member churches to attend the meetings of the central committee, providing a possibility for formal and informal discussions. The general secretary of the SACC, John Rees, a Methodist layman, played an important role of liaison, but his views were often considered to be one-sided, representing white leaders of churches the majority of whose members were black.

The 1971 central committee meeting in Addis Ababa provided the first opportunity to test the views of the member churches on the grants made by the Special Fund. It turned out that there was considerable support for the WCC's policy — and not only from churches in the so-called third world. Committee members from North America, Western and Eastern Europe were on the whole supportive, as was the Russian Orthodox Church. But there were questions, chiefly about three issues: (1) Did the WCC by its actions support violence? (2) Why were grants made without control of the manner in which they were spent? (3) Should the WCC risk one-sidedness by concentrating so much of its attention on the racial issue on southern Africa? After full discussion the central committee responded clearly. The most crucial statement was on the issue of violence. The committee said that

> the churches must always stand for the liberation of the oppressed and of victims of violent measures which deny basic human rights. It calls attention to the fact that violence is in many cases inherent in the maintenance of the status quo. Nevertheless, the WCC does not and cannot identify itself completely with any political movement, nor does it pass judgement on those victims of racism who are driven to violence as the only way left to them to redress grievances and so open the way for a new and more just social order. [7]

This motion, adopted without dissent and with no recorded abstentions, helped to put the grants by the Special Fund into perspective. Reaction to the PCR grants by the so-called historic peace churches — who condemn any form of violence — was one of understanding and support, while representatives of some of the churches with a history of supporting national wars were strongly opposed to supporting the liberation movements.

Equally important was the decision at Addis Ababa to implement what was known as "the Martin Luther King resolution" adopted at the Uppsala assembly, calling for non-violent methods of achieving social change. The committee identified six key issues for a WCC study on violence and non-violence:

— the meaning of power in the light of human experience and Christian convictions about love and justice;
— the dimensions of "violence";
— the necessity of and limitation upon the state's use of "violence" as a preservative against anarchy;
— the relationship between conflict and reconciliation;
— the search for more adequate models of the humane society as goals for social change; and
— the extent to which the churches as institutions should identify themselves with or against any of the parties involved in social conflict. [8]

The committee also spoke out against the sale of arms to South Africa in cablegrams to the British prime minister and the president of the Organization of African Unity (OAU). Informed that all organizations appealing for grants from the Special Fund had indicated that they would not use the grants for military purposes but for activities in harmony with the purposes of the WCC, the committee initiated a new appeal to the member churches to support the Special Fund financially. Finally, it laid the basis for further policy and action by instructing the staff to begin an immediate study and analysis of the involvement of the WCC and member churches in the perpetuation of racism by investment policies and practices.

Meanwhile, an increasing number of local ecumenical groups and churches, particularly in the Federal Republic of Germany and the Netherlands, was beginning to support the PCR and its Special Fund. Negative reactions to PCR by some church bodies had made such groups more aware of their own responsibility. Heart-warming signs of solidarity were received in Geneva. The impressive thing was that, at the height of the attacks on the Council and its member churches, there was a substantial rise in contributions to the Special Fund. This increase in support, coming from churches as well as from people and organizations that had never had any previous contact with the ecumenical movement, has been sustained since then.

The local groundswell in different parts of Europe provided many unexpected additional opportunities to awaken people's consciousness to the real conditions of apartheid. Several Roman Catholic dioceses in the Netherlands participated in fund-raising. Many local ecumenical action groups and some secular groups started information campaigns and put considerable pressure on church assemblies and synods to speak out forcefully in favour of the WCC's actions and to reject the lies of South African propaganda. It became evident that parishioners did not all fit the stereotype some church leaders had of their members: often they were well ahead of their leaders in understanding the issues at stake. This healthy development bore its fruits. The churches at all levels were forced to grapple with the issues involved.

Money matters

The Fund was a symbolic action. It was a sign, necessary to express something greater than itself. It was intended to set something in motion. And this is what began to happen when the PCR made its next move on disinvestment by the WCC and the member churches.

Already in 1969 the WCC finance committee had approved a directive to its investment managers, expressing the desire that the WCC portfolio be built on investments in concerns engaged in locally constructive activities. It therefore decided that no resources should be invested in concerns which were wholly or primarily engaged in producing or handling armaments or activities in or trade with South Africa and Rhodesia. A joint document from the commissions of the WCC Divisions of Inter-Church Aid, Refugee and World Service and World Mission and Evangelism, adopted in November 1970, called for special attention to how investment policies of mission and service agencies "affect southern Africa, and other areas in the world, including racial and deprived minorities within their own countries".

In 1971 the commission of the PCR requested a thorough investigation of the portfolio of investments owned by the WCC in order to discover any direct or indirect investment in companies and banks operating in southern Africa as well as any investment in subsidiary companies operating in that region. It asked member churches to do likewise. PCR's conviction was that Christians must not abdicate ethical responsibility for the outcome of economic policies. The impact of foreign economic support to racist and apartheid structures was seen to involve moral decisions which should not be avoided — or left to technicians alone. Having little experience of its own in this field, PCR turned to the US churches and asked for their help, since they had already acted in this area. Of considerable assistance was an outstanding study of Western investment in apartheid by Ruth First and others.[9]

In 1972 the PCR put its proposals to the WCC central committee meeting in Utrecht. By an overwhelming majority, the committee instructed the WCC's finance committee to sell forthwith existing holdings and to make no further investments in corporations involved in or trading with South Africa, Namibia, Zimbabwe (then still Rhodesia), Angola, Mozambique and Guinea-Bissau and to deposit none of its funds in banks which maintained direct banking operations in these countries. Member churches, Christian agencies and individual Christians outside southern Africa were urged to use their influence, including stockholders action and disinvestment, to press corporations to withdraw from these countries.

The central question in the debate at Utrecht was whether to advocate the complete withdrawal of multinationals from southern Africa or a reform of their policies, for instance through codes of conduct. The Evangelical Church in Germany (EKD) recommended that everything should be done to avoid more tension and that the churches should refrain from outside economic pressure. Instead they proposed working for improved conditions for black workers in foreign companies and so to stay within the legal framework of southern Africa. The proposal was clearly an alternative to that of the PCR but it claimed to work towards the same goal: justice for the racially oppressed. In the end, the Utrecht resolution opted for the radical approach of withdrawal, but the EKD proposal was mentioned in a footnote to the decision in the context of "multiple strategies". Also, a distinction was made between the WCC's decision to sell its own shares and the recommendation that member churches use all their influence, including shareholder action, to persuade companies to withdraw. The WCC clearly wanted to set the example, but it realized that not all the churches could be expected to follow because of their different national contexts.

Not surprisingly, multinational corporations made statements against the WCC policy, citing remarks by Chief Gatsha Buthelezi and other Bantustan leaders as evidence that black workers were opposed to disinvestment because it would lead to massive unemployment. According to these leaders, the WCC was in fact advocating the "pauperization" of black people in order to drive them to revolution. Similar arguments were also used by several member churches, especially in Britain, West Germany and Switzerland (see Chapter 5). But the WCC and a growing number of member churches saw their policy as a last attempt to bring about non-violent change. And they in turn quoted the SACC, church leaders like Desmond Tutu and Allan Boesak and the liberation movements to make their point.

Whatever the outcome of the investment debate in church synods, assemblies and commissions, the WCC decision, like the grants to liberation movements by the Special Fund, provoked intense discussions. Again, these were often stimulated and forced on the agenda by grassroots ecumenical groups. But in the case of investments, more basic and wider questions were at stake. In a background document for the 1973 central committee meeting, the PCR wrote that the disinvestment decision indicated

> a further move on the part of the WCC as a whole towards its involvement in the struggle for racial justice. In many ways, the decision on a withdrawal of investment is of much more fundamental importance than the preceding one on the grants, because it questions fundamentally the social, economic and political structures of both the West and southern Africa.

For the churches this raised the whole question of the roots and consequences of the capitalist system in their own countries, and their links with that system.

Less controversial was the recommendation from the Utrecht meeting calling on the WCC and the churches to campaign against white migration to southern Africa. It was generally agreed that efforts by the South African government to encourage white immigration were aimed at perpetuating and strengthening the existing racist structures. The large influx of white skilled personnel created additional black unemployment and kept the black population at the lower end of the job scale. Bishop Zulu expressed his wholehearted support, and the resolution was adopted without opposition. As a result many churches in Europe, in particular, actively supported campaigns to stop emigration to South Africa.

White South Africa had become a focus for WCC concern, not least because it was explaining its ideology and behaviour in terms of its vision of Christian civilization. In the process, the WCC came to see that action with a specific and well-defined focus usually stands a far better chance of achieving its aims than responses which are general. The debate on disinvestment had made this clear, and the WCC's naming of corporations directly involved in investment in or trade with southern Africa had the desired effect. Churches and ecumenical groups outside the region now had a lever to put pressure on them to start shareholder action and to check their own investment portfolios. The discussion this provoked within the churches about the ethics and stewardship of investment went far beyond the apartheid debate.

A process of liberation

The meeting of the central committee in 1973 in Geneva provided an occasion for the WCC to restate that by its the very nature a programme of the churches to combat racism is involved in a process of liberation, not only of the oppressed but also of the oppressors. Both needed to be liberated from fear and guilt and for a shared life in community, justice, mutual respect and trust. In this way they could become authentic persons, able to fulfil their capacities as human beings.

The meeting in Geneva also provided the first occasion since the PCR was launched for meetings with representatives of the South African churches, who attended the central committee as "representatives of member churches not otherwise represented". Since it had proved impossible to meet in South Africa itself because of the conditions set by Vorster, this was a second-best solution to the problem of communication. The meetings, held outside the normal programme, were also attended by several members of the central committee and the PCR commission. WCC staff included two members from South Africa: Brigalia Bam and Desmond Tutu.

The discussions got off to a difficult start. The fact that it had taken three years to have a meeting of this kind complicated the situation, at least in the beginning. Both sides reiterated their positions. But not all South Africans were of the same opinion; and some preferred not to speak. Nor were the WCC representatives unanimous in their positions. The occasion did however help to clarify many misunderstandings. On the grants and the disinvestment issue people continued to disagree. For the South Africans attending, it became clear that the WCC was trying to respond to the needs of the oppressed and that every initiative was fully documented and debated by the responsible bodies of the Council.

The 1973 central committee also commended to the member churches a statement on violence, non-violence and the struggle for social justice. The document centred on new perceptions of the problem, and stated that it is not only a right but the duty of Christians to oppose any unlawful power on behalf of the poor and the oppressed. But the use of violence or force in this connection was handled with caution. The statement referred to three earlier discussions on violence: the 1948 Amsterdam assembly, where the issue was participation in war, the 1966 Church and Society conference, which focused on the problem of revolutionary violence against oppressive social systems, and the 1968 Uppsala assembly, which brought into focus both the violence of the status quo and the significance of non-violent methods of social change.

The 1973 statement moved away from the "just war" concept to set the whole issue in the wider context of the struggle for social justice, as it affects both oppressors and oppressed. Concrete illustrations, including one from South Africa, were given of the dilemmas facing Christians. In recent years, examples of new and sophisticated non-violent movements for justice and freedom, like those led by Gandhi and Martin Luther King, had inspired the world and the churches.

The study made three observations which bore directly on the situation in South Africa:

a) there are some forms of violence in which Christians may not participate and which the churches must condemn...: the conquest of one people by another or the deliberate oppression of one class or race by another, which offend divine justice;

b) too little attention has been given by the church and by resistance movements to the methods and techniques of non-violence;

c) we reject some facile assumptions about non-violence which have been current in the recent debate. Non-violent action is highly political. It may be extremely controversial. [10]

While the 1973 statement included significant reservations on the right to violent resistance, even as a last resort, the WCC was careful not to tell anyone what to do in a situation of unendurable violence.

In 1974, the central committee meeting in West Berlin made its next move, this time concentrating on banks making loans to the South African government and its agencies — the most direct and eloquent vote in favour of apartheid a non-South African could make. The WCC knew it had to choose its course very carefully, because important issues were at stake and the international financial world was watching with deep concern, ready to attack any mistake or misjudgement by the WCC.

In its action on banks, the WCC decided to concentrate largely, though not exclusively, on the European-American Banking Corporation (EABC) and its member banks. EABC had a unique connection with South Africa. It made substantial credit arrangements and a concerted effort to assist the government of South Africa in overcoming its serious economic and financial problems. The WCC sent an explanatory document to the EABC and its members soliciting assurances that they would stop granting loans to the South African government and its agencies. If satisfactory assurances were not forthcoming, no more WCC funds would be deposited with these banks. At the same time, the WCC urged all member churches to use their influence to press these and other banks participating in loans to stop doing so.

In a letter to one of the EABC members, the AMRO Bank in the Netherlands, the WCC wrote:

> The essential function of a bank we believe, is to administer capital, in liquid or quasi-liquid form. Capital itself is morally neutral, because only a society

which consumed everything it produced could avoid the accumulation of capital (whether liquid or in fixed assets), and such a society would betray future generations. What can never be morally neutral, however, is the use to which capital is put. So while banking as an activity is common to many human societies, the particular policies which it chooses to adopt are a proper object of moral judgement... Because it is central to the gospel that faith without works is dead, churches individually — and as grouped in the WCC — owe their primary loyalty not to their own members but to the Lord of the oikoumene, the whole inhabited earth... This has some very concrete practical implications for the World Council... [The WCC has] to see that any capital for which it has responsibility is used for its God-given purpose. That purpose is not the accumulation of more capital, but self-giving service in the name of its self-giving Lord. The message of the gospel is unmistakeable on this point: Christians are specifically enjoined not to lay up treasure on earth, but to use what they have to seek the kingdom of God on earth... So capital is for WCC a means, while for AMRO, it appears to be an end in itself.[11]

The correspondence with the banks brought into the open the issue of public accountability, an issue which neither the banks nor the churches had faced in such an acute form. It highlighted the usefulness of multiple strategies, including discussions with banks as well as boycotts and closing bank accounts, the importance of the educational aspect of ecumenical action and the need for strategies to combat racism on an institutional and not just an individual level. The banking issue showed that racism can be no less real when its roots are in supposedly neutral structures run by people without racial prejudice.

The WCC realized that the growing unwillingness in banking circles to continue heavy involvement in South Africa was obviously dictated by considerations of commercial prudence. At the same time, however, it hoped and believed that there were more fundamental reasons for the banks' second thoughts.

A Christian witness

In 1975 PCR and the WCC Faith and Order Commission co-sponsored a consultation on Racism in Theology. In exploring the Christian witness against racism, participants discussed collective repentance in corporate action and reflection, the struggle against racism and the search for a just society, the role of the church and discipleship and disciplined life. It said, among other things:

We dare not brand racism as sin without at once responding to it with real and practical penitence. This response involves repentance both at the individual level and at the corporate level, and repentance commits us to action. The two elements are intimately connected, which is why we prefer to speak of repentance-action or penitent action. But what is the appropriate action?

Some, we know, define repentance in terms of compensatory action. We hesitate to adopt this solution, however, mainly because no material compensation could possibly repair all the immeasurable harm done in the past. To call for compensation in this sense would only be to belittle the suffering which has been caused. [12]

This statement clearly tried to address the question of reparations which had been dramatically raised at the 1969 Notting Hill consultation and remained high on the agenda, especially of the US churches as they tried to cope with racism and the emergence of Black Power.

The WCC consultation expressed the conviction that compensatory action had to be forward- rather than backward-looking, concerned with a new and more just future, and proposed four criteria which would do justice to the still more radical imperatives of the gospel:

a) Ideally, the action should not be unilateral, but decided by both parties, oppressors and oppressed, together.

b) It should open up the possibility of real community in the future.

c) It should be related to the wider area of racism in the secular and political field.

d) Adherence to these criteria will be costly. [13]

Seven years after Uppsala, the Nairobi Assembly in 1975 had to review all WCC programmes, including the Programme to Combat Racism. Before participants left for Kenya, they received a letter from the WCC officers about visiting South Africa before or after the assembly. The letter reminded them that the South African government was selective in allowing Christian leaders to visit the country and banned WCC central committee members and staff. "... At a time when the assembly is bound to express itself on the situation in southern Africa," the letter said, "the possibility of making meaningful contact with Africans will be even more unlikely... In the interest of solidarity, you should seriously consider whether it is appropriate to visit South Africa immediately before or after the assembly, even if you receive permission to do so." Attached to the letter was a moving appeal from a South African in exile:

Your presence in South Africa will be a continuous reminder to every black you see of the privileges they are denied daily. You will have freedom of movement and association. You will be able to use buses and elevators and restaurants forbidden to blacks. In short, you will be treated as a person. What is it that you come to see in South Africa?... Do you come to see if the blacks are still suffering? Is that something you must see with your own eyes before you'll believe it?... We often noticed how "fact-finding" trips by church leaders have been used either by the South African government for propaganda or by church spokespersons to discredit our liberation movements and our true leaders. This hurts. If you care, please refuse to go. Do so as an act of solidarity with 80 percent of South Africa's people, who have no freedom of travel in their own land. [14]

In the context of ever-greater determination among the peoples of the world to participate in decision-making and in efforts towards self-reliance, racism was one of several issues that came in for lively debate at Nairobi. Bishop Philip Russell from South Africa moved a resolution that the churches should not support the PCR unless assurances were given that the Special Fund would give no assistance to organizations using violence. His motion was lost by a considerable majority. Burgess Carr, general secretary of the AACC, expressed the gratitude of the African churches to all outside Africa who had supported the PCR and so helped to give credibility to the churches' efforts on the continent.

In 1976 the WCC central committee grappled with the issue of South Africa's Bantustans. This was directly related to the decision by the South African government that year to proclaim the Transkei "independent" as the "national home" of the Xhosa-speaking Africans in the country. Pretoria had set up a vast campaign to promote international recognition of the area. It wanted to have the Transkei admitted to the United Nations as the first of nine "homelands", and hoped Western nations would recognize the Transkei and increase foreign investments.

In preparation for the debate PCR published a booklet on the government's Bantustan policy and its consequences for the people who were to live in these badly eroded tracts of land. [15] The study concluded that the Bantustan policy was not a new departure in the granting of self-determination, but a new means to serve the political and economic interests of the white people. Bantustans would become a permanent reservoir of black migrant labour, dependent on the needs of the white economy. Politically, international acceptance would mean acceptance of the white claim that blacks could enjoy full civic rights and equality within the present South African state. Bantustans would be the logical conclusion of the policy of separate development.

During the debate in the central committee, David J.X. Gqweta argued that withholding recognition from the Transkei would cause even more suffering for its people, and he asked the WCC to help them in some way. But the committee, while expressing solidarity with the Xhosa-speaking people as they struggled for the legitimate rights of all Africans, condemned the South African government for an action that would make three million South Africans foreigners in their own country and called on all member churches and governments to oppose the Bantustan policy and to withhold recognition of the Transkei as an independent state.

From South Africa itself came the grim news of yet another massacre. In an uprising in Soweto in 1976 at least 300 children had been killed by the South African police (the official death toll was 176 children). The episode followed several months of growing tension over the insistence by the Department of Bantu Education that English and Afrikaans should be equally used for instruction in black primary and high schools. The students refused to accept this, and between ten and twenty thousand children organized a protest march, to which the police and troops reacted by opening fire on the crowds. The SACC commented that the involvement of schoolchildren in the confrontation had "the frightening implication that black grievances are not only a matter of politics but have become a matter of intense and widespread agony felt even by children, which could escalate into a national catastrophe". Describing this as a manifestation of the new momentum of the struggle for freedom and dignity in South Africa, the central committee called on the regime to end violence against the oppressed majority, to recognize their full human rights and to release all those imprisoned for political reasons.

Despite this and similar exhortations from the churches and the international community, the situation in South Africa deteriorated daily. On 12 September 1977 Steve Biko died in police custody, and on 19 October of that same year eighteen organizations and a number of individuals were banned by the South African government, including the Christian Institute of Southern Africa and its director, Beyers Naudé. Strong statements of condemnation came from around the world. The PCR published a background discussion paper entitled *South Africa's Hope — What Price Now?*, raising sharp questions about the options which remained open after the latest developments. The paper refuted as fraudulent the comparison by the Vorster government of black resistance in South Africa with terrorism in Europe. Instead it asked for a recognition of the rebellion in the country against the regime, quoting a black South African who lived through the June 1976 Soweto uprising: "I was in Soweto when the police came in. I saw them shoot an eight-year-old child dead in the street. And you ask me to be non-violent?" Three effective ways for action were recommended in the paper: providing support to refugees, building support for those working for liberation inside South Africa and working to end all foreign support to South Africa.

A grant by the Special Fund in 1978 to the Patriotic Front of Zimbabwe caused widespread concern and brought several member churches to a near-breaking point with the WCC. The grant was released only a few days before one of the Front's partners, the Zimbabwe African People's Union (ZAPU), shot down a Rhodesian airliner, killing all passengers. Newspaper headlines critical of the WCC surfaced again. As a result one member church, the Presbyterian Church of Ireland, withdrew from the Council, while the Evangelical Lutheran Church of Schaumburg-Lippe, smallest of the provincial churches in the Evangelical Church in Germany, suspended its membership. The Salvation Army first suspended its membership and later accepted fraternal status with the WCC as a Christian World Communion.

Other member churches realized that the liberation war in Rhodesia was reaching its climax. Cruelties of many kinds took place, including the killing of white missionaries. Many of these atrocities were perpetrated by the so-called Selous Scouts, a special unit of the white-led Rhodesian army. The WCC, through the PCR, participated in and contributed towards the negotiations for independence. The Lancaster House Agreement in 1979 ended the civil war and transferred power to representatives of the Zimbabwean majority in 1980. The stand taken by the WCC was finally vindicated.

Meanwhile, the worsening situation in southern Africa as a whole prompted the WCC's Commission on Inter-Church Aid, Refugee and World Service (CICARWS) to increase its activities and to launch a special appeal for US$5 million for the region. The human suffering and distress resulting from the conflicts and the liberation struggle presented a major challenge for the ecumenical fellowship. The proceeds of the appeal were channelled through national councils of churches, individual churches and in some cases through non-church groups and liberation movements.

Other parts of the WCC, especially the scholarship programme and the graduate school of the Ecumenical Institute at Bossey, invited white South African students to share in their programmes and exposed them to ecumenical and liberation theologies. The Commission on World Mission and Evangelism (CWME) arranged several consultations with representatives of Protestant and Roman Catholic missions involved in southern Africa to analyze developments there and to formulate concrete recommendations for action in often delicate situations.

Taking stock

After ten years of combating racism through the PCR, WCC general secretary Philip Potter suggested in 1979 that the member churches and the WCC itself should take stock of their past involvement and analyze and list their priorities for the 1980s. A worldwide process of consultation developed over a period of eighteen months, in which churches, national and regional councils of churches and organizations of the racially oppressed and action groups from all continents participated enthusiastically. This major exercise culminated in a world consultation on Racism in the 1980s, held in Noordwijkerhout, the Netherlands, in 1980.

A sizeable representation from South Africa attended the meeting. At one point they held a closed session to discuss and orchestrate their own point of view. It was clear that they were in a dangerous position. They knew that voting in favour of sanctions could mean arrest upon return home. In the end they did not need to do this because the other consultation participants voted unanimously for comprehensive sanctions.

Oliver Tambo had been invited as a keynote speaker, but due to illness was replaced by ANC general secretary Alfred Nzo. He and others made it clear that the organizations receiving support through the Special Fund did not see this instrument in monetary terms only but as a way of dramatizing and internationalizing their struggle.

The hope of the organizers of the consultation was that critics of the WCC's position on racism would be sufficiently represented to enable a broad and constructive discussion on ecumenical involvement for the next ten years. As it turned out, few of the critics came, partly perhaps because by that time Zimbabwe had just become independent and Robert Mugabe, president of ZANU, was elected its first prime minister. In fact much of the old debate on grants had been overtaken by events. Mugabe, whom South African propaganda had branded as a "terrorist", was suddenly depicted in the Western media as a democratic and Christian leader.

Considerable attention was given at the consultation to the role of the media and South African government propaganda efforts to discredit the WCC. Since the grants to liberation movements, a host of organizations — the Christian League of Southern Africa (CLSA), the Rhodesia Christian Group (RCG), the Christian Affirmation League, the International Christian Network (ICN), the Club of Ten, the International Society for Human Rights and others — had attacked the SACC and the WCC. What was less known was the extent to which the South African government was directly or indirectly involved in several of these and other organizations and projects. One of its specific aims was to influence church affairs inside and outside South Africa. The methods used included personal contacts, financial aid, conferences, advertisements and publications. The best organized was probably the CLSA, whose goal was "to influence all churches to withdraw and dissociate themselves from the WCC and SACC — seen to be a major source of ungodly doctrine and action infiltrating the churches". Its chairman, the Rev. Fred Shaw, spoke of the "theological justification of violence and terror within our churches and the tendency of synods to regard doctrinal matters as trivial in relation to such matters as the affirmation of the WCC support for black liberation organizations and 'terrorism'".[16]

Although the English-speaking churches in South Africa would have nothing to do with it, the CLSA grew and appeared to have strong financial backing, though Shaw refused to reveal his sources of support. The CLSA worked closely with the Rhodesia Christian Group, led by Arthur Lewis, an Anglican priest, senator in Ian Smith's parliament and crusader against "terrorism", who said that "through the WCC and its ancillaries, terror has been given the stamp of respectability".[17]

Several of these organizations with extreme right-wing connections in Europe and North America created the ICN as a loose network to oppose the WCC more effectively. Its chairman was Peter Beyerhaus, professor of mission and ecumenical studies in Tübingen, Germany, a former missionary in South Africa and an outspoken critic of the WCC.

The South African Foundation, established in 1959, claimed to be independent and financed by private enterprise. From its offices in Paris, London, Bonn and Washington it sought to maintain investor confidence in South Africa and regularly sponsored tours for key decision-makers in both industry and the churches. Church leaders from West Germany, in particular, were invited by the Foundation and with some success.

The vicious attacks by so-called Christian groups against the WCC and its member churches frightened some church members. But it became clear that these were not spontaneous protests as they at first appeared. They were part of a well-orchestrated propaganda campaign directed largely by the South African government. There is no doubt that the apartheid regime became alarmed by the seriousness with which the churches conducted their programmes, and decisions to counter South Africa's growing isolation were taken at the highest level in the government. The world consultation alerted the WCC to the methods used by the regime in launching smear campaigns aimed at discrediting the Council. And it urged the churches to refute such allegations and redress the bias in the media by producing counter-information.

A shared commitment

Welcoming the report of the consultation, the central committee meeting in 1980 strongly reaffirmed the PCR and its Special Fund and concluded that the situation in South Africa and Namibia needed the further special attention of the churches. It declared that

> apartheid is a sin which as a fundamental matter of faith is to be rejected as a perversion of the Christian gospel (this may be expressed in terms of a covenant, status confessionis or equivalent commitment).

Furthermore, it called on the member churches to

press governments and international organizations to enforce comprehensive
sanctions against South Africa, including a withdrawal of investments, an end
to bank loans, arms embargo and oil sanctions and in general for the isolation
of the state of South Africa;

and to

cease any direct, and as far as possible indirect, financial involvement in
activities which support the apartheid regime. [18]

It was evident that increased awareness of the apartheid system had
sharpened the WCC's position. At the same time, the SACC and the
member churches in South Africa were becoming more and more
involved in the struggle, and the fellowship with them was growing.

Another important consequence of the consultation process was to
make the churches and councils of churches aware of their more direct
responsibilities in combating racism, both at home and abroad, through
policies and programmes of their own. PCR had helped to internationalize
the struggle of the racially oppressed by making the churches conscious of
this; the future role of the WCC and the PCR would be less as initiator
than as monitor, supporter and mediator in local, national and regional
initiatives. The 1980 meeting signalled an end to ten crucial years in
which the WCC was in an almost continuously exposed position, taking
in tow its member churches on issues of racism and apartheid. It had
begun to do so at a time when most of its constituency was unwilling to
face racism head-on. But the cry of the oppressed could no longer be
ignored. A strong response was needed.

The year 1981 was important for the WCC in its relations with the
banks in which it had deposits. This followed an extensive correspondence with the EABC and its members in 1974 and the publication
in 1979 of a UN report on bank loans to South Africa. The WCC
developed a list of carefully defined criteria for assessing the involvement of its own banks active in South Africa. These were adopted by
the executive committee in February 1981 and conveyed to the banks
concerned.

On 15 September 1981, Philip Potter held a press conference during
which he explained the WCC's position and announced that it was
terminating its relationships with three major banks: Dresdner Bank,
Swiss Bank Corporation (SBS) and the Union Bank of Switzerland
(UBS). Thus the WCC was putting its own house in order by taking
decisions which matched its policy statements. In so doing, Potter said,
the WCC was not in any way criticizing the services rendered to the WCC
by these banks, nor the employees of these banks, some of whom
belonged to member churches, but only the policy these banks followed
in relation to South Africa. The breaking of relations was in order to

"express the WCC's full support for the liberation of South Africa from the system of racism embodied in apartheid".

At the WCC Vancouver assembly in 1983 the churches showed that they were in no mood to retreat from earlier commitments, which had stemmed not from passing fads but from the very heart of the gospel. There was no backing away from the PCR, which had become a symbol of ecumenical social engagement. The active participation of Desmond Tutu, then general secretary of the SACC, Allan Boesak and several representatives of the ANC (including Alfred Nzo and Thabo Mbeki) provided a special opportunity to consider anew developments in South Africa. The public interventions of the South African church leaders reflected enormous courage in speaking out on issues in spite of personal threats and restrictions laid down by the regime. Boesak, one of the centre-stage figures in the struggle between church and state in the 1980s, presented an eloquent keynote address on the main theme, "Jesus Christ — the Life of the World":

> In South Africa apartheid and injustice still reign supreme. Inequality is still sanctified by law and racial superiority is still justified by theology. Today, with the blatant support of so many Western governments, apartheid seems stronger than ever and the dream of justice and human dignity for South Africa's black people more remote than ever. In our world, it is not the joyful, hopeful sound of the word of life that is being heard. No, that word is drowned by the ugly sound of gunfire, by the screams of our children and the endless cry of the powerless: How long, Lord?[19]

In his report as general secretary, Potter put the issue of racism in the context of the biblical vision of living stones. "Believers, as living stones," he said, "overcome the separations of racism and become the true human race made in the image of God... All are the people of God as a sign of God's plan to unite all peoples into one human family in justice and peace."[20]

The delegates recognized that substantial progress had been made in the churches' commitment to racial justice. Some churches had begun to deepen their understanding of the root causes of racism. There was a recognition that racism is strongly interrelated with sexism, economic exploitation, class domination and militarism and that overcoming all of these is part of the same struggle.

The race debate at the assembly took place against the background of increasing South African government pressure on churches and in particular on the SACC. In 1981 the government had ordered an investigation into the SACC by the Eloff Commission, initially in response to alleged financial irregularities. However, it was soon clear that the commission had received a much broader mandate and was being asked to examine the inception, development, objectives and activities of the council as well as the organizations and people involved in its financial support. Early in 1983 a delegation of international church leaders had gone to South Africa to appear before the Eloff Commission and to testify about their experiences with the work of the SACC.

In the light of this dangerous situation, the Vancouver assembly expressed its admiration and support for the prophetic and courageous stand for human dignity, justice and liberation taken by the SACC. Its statement on southern Africa said: "As a consequence of the life and witness of the Christians and churches, there is unrelenting pressure on them and the SACC, most recently shown in the activities of the Eloff Commission which appears to be an effort to muzzle and destroy the SACC."[21] On 15 February 1984, the Eloff Commission presented its report to the South African parliament. It made harsh criticisms of the SACC, calling it revolutionary, destabilizing, secretive and confrontational. It said that economic sabotage as an offence would have to be defined and the SACC's administration of donated funds brought under control of the Fund Raising Act. But the Commission did not recommend any action against the SACC in terms of the Affected Organisation Act.

The WCC executive committee rejected the conclusions of the Eloff Commission, drawing particular attention to its distorted understanding of church-state relations and to the SACC's ministry through humanitarian assistance and prophetic witness against oppression. The central committee decided at its meeting in 1984 that southern Africa would remain a priority for the PCR. It stated that the accords South Africa had made with Angola and Mozambique had created a false and misleading impression that South Africa was now embarking on a policy of establishing peace in the region. The committee also condemned the government's so-called constitutional proposals as fraudulent and racist because they still did not provide for real sharing of power and excluded blacks entirely from the political process. Forced removals of people from "black spots" were causing even greater hardship among the black population.

A new mood

During 1985 and 1986 the situation in South Africa deteriorated even further. The government of President P.W. Botha declared two states of emergency. Tens of thousands of people were detained, many under the age of 20. Hundreds were beaten, tortured and killed. The South African authorities imposed a strict censorship on foreign media, hoping to silence international criticism. But internal opposition to apartheid was not broken, and the struggle for liberation intensified.

At this point in the history of South Africa, a dramatic international ecumenical response was needed; and in December 1985, twenty-five years after Cottesloe, the WCC and SACC together organized an emergency meeting in Harare, Zimbabwe, between world church leaders and leaders of the churches in South Africa to deal with the volatile situation within the country and South Africa's increasingly aggressive efforts at destabilization in the frontline states. Some 85 people were present.

In deeply moving testimonies, South African delegates told harrowing stories of police brutality, torture, detentions, beating and killings. They appealed for moral and material help in their hour of great need. One delegate asked, "Why must our liberation come at the cost of four year olds being shot by bullets?" The tragedy, he and others stated, was that most young blacks were not only saying that they had had enough of apartheid but that they were no longer afraid to die in their struggle to end it. For young people education was no longer a priority. Liberation was. Church leaders who continually advised non-violence and called for peaceful solutions were increasingly being dismissed as irrelevant. "How does one preach reconciliation with those who refuse to negotiate with the leaders of the people?", they asked.

The Harare meeting brought together for the first time church leaders from inside and outside South Africa in a significant way to discuss what ministry and witness meant in South Africa. The South Africans asked unambiguously for the imposition of comprehensive and mandatory sanctions against their country. The usual Western argument that sanctions would hurt the blacks most was no longer accepted as valid. One South African participant said, "If you don't support sanctions now, the next time we meet we will say, 'Give us guns'."[22]

The meeting responded with a call for concerted pressure on the Pretoria regime by the international community. Strong pleas were to intensify the campaign for effective economic sanctions. While recognizing that sanctions were costly to the people of South Africa, the participants noted that they were "ready to bear this cost to bring closer the day of liberation". The meeting also advocated special economic assistance to the frontline states and humanitarian programmes for people most affected within South Africa.

The main recommendations of the Harare meeting were endorsed by the WCC executive committee at its meeting in Kinshasa in 1986. Later that year, the WCC, together with the World Alliance of Reformed Churches (WARC), Lutheran World Federation (LWF) and World Young Women's Christian Association (YWCA), held another meeting in Harare. This one brought together some 90 young people, most from

South Africa, Namibia and the frontline states. Several of the South African participants were arrested upon their return home.

The WCC was now working in close cooperation with WARC and LWF in monitoring events in South Africa and taking action. Background information and joint statements were prepared for the day of prayer for South Africa on 16 June 1986 to mark the tenth anniversary of the Soweto uprisings. Dame Nita Barrow, one of the WCC presidents, and Archbishop Ted Scott, former moderator of the central committee, were members of a Commonwealth Eminent Persons Group which visited South Africa in 1986.

Later that year, another WCC president, Archbishop Walter Makhulu, himself a South African, and two WCC staff members were able to enter South Africa for the consecration of Desmond Tutu as Anglican archbishop of Cape Town. As a result of these visits and a specific request by the SACC for as many visits as possible by WCC officials, the WCC executive committee decided that visits to South Africa and Namibia by committee members, commissioners and WCC staff should now be encouraged, provided that they were made at the specific invitation of the SACC, the Council of Churches in Namibia (CCN), a WCC member church in one of the two countries or an organization recognized by the WCC as representative of the struggle for liberation. [23]

A growing influence

As the national and international influence of the liberation movements in South Africa and Namibia was growing, the WCC decided it was time for a major encounter between their leaders and representatives of its member churches. That meeting took place in Lusaka, Zambia, in 1987, under the theme "The Struggle for Justice is the Struggle for Peace". It addressed in particular the issues of violence and communism in the struggle against apartheid. Some 250 delegates participated, including 42 from South Africa and 28 from Namibia.

In South Africa a continuing state of emergency had resulted in virtual martial law. Incursions into the frontline states had escalated. Just ten days prior to the meeting, South African planes bombed the Zambian town of Livingstone, killing four civilians. The Lusaka statement and action plan, drafted after intense discussions, was a strong document which moved beyond the Harare declaration of 1985. Theologically and politically, it affirmed the right of the people of southern Africa to secure justice and peace through their liberation movements. It stated:

It is our belief that civil authority is instituted of God to do good and that under the biblical imperative all people are obliged to do justice and show special care for the oppressed and the poor. It is this understanding that leaves us with no alternative but to conclude that the South African regime and its colonial domination of Namibia is illegitimate. We recognize that the people of South Africa and Namibia, who are yearning for justice and peace, have identified the liberation movements of their countries to be the authentic vehicles that express their aspirations for self-determination. [24]

The meeting thus called on the churches to strengthen their contacts with the liberation movements and asked the WCC to send a delegation of eminent church persons on a mission to the US, UK, Germany, Japan, the European Community, permanent member states of the UN Security Council and the Contact Group of Nations on Namibia. The role of such a mission would be to put pressure on governments, trade unions, churches and multinationals to see that UN and WCC resolutions recommending a complete isolation of South Africa were implemented. The WCC was asked to embark on a campaign to expose the moral and theological illegitimacy of the South African regime by encouraging its member churches to recognize, support and relate to the liberation movements. The meeting concluded that:

> While remaining committed to peaceful change, we recognize that the nature of the South African regime, which wages war against its own inhabitants and neighbours, compels the movements to the use of force along with other means to end oppression. [25]

This statement probably went as far as the churches could go together in expressing understanding of the armed struggle in South Africa. They were confronted with the question as to which form of violence is less evil: the violence of the white oppressors as a means to defend their privileges or the counter-violence employed by the oppressed blacks as a strategy of liberation. The issue faced at the Lusaka meeting was summarized succinctly by Charles Villa-Vicencio: "The church can never be synonymous with a particular liberation movement, but it is theologically obliged to share in the liberation process."[26] And in the ecumenical movement outside South Africa, a growing number of churches were forced to move, however reluctantly and cautiously, beyond moral outrage and theological critique to engage in viable programmes of action. The Lusaka statement was subsequently adopted by the SACC, though some of its member churches were shaken and did not support its conclusions.

The Lusaka meeting also served another important purpose: it provided an opportunity for South African church representatives to meet exiled liberation movement leaders after many years of separation and a lack of communication. A symbolic high point came when Oliver Tambo and Beyers Naudé met each other for the first time and warmly embraced.

Church leaders from South Africa and abroad, particularly from the USA and Western Europe, were profoundly impressed by the responsible attitude and creative contribution made by the liberation movement leaders. They became aware that the typical portrayal of these people by the media as communists and terrorists was false and needed to be corrected at home.

Soon afterwards, the WCC executive committee endorsed the Lusaka proposals and mandated an Eminent Church Persons Group (ECPG) to make an ultimate effort to lobby Western governments and Japan for full and compulsory sanctions as the last remaining non-violent means to avert a bloodbath in South Africa. The group, headed by the former president of Zimbabwe Canaan Banana, started its work in 1989, two years after the mission of the Commonwealth Eminent Persons Group to South Africa, which after strenuous efforts had concluded that the South African government was "not yet prepared to negotiate fundamental change". The ECPG mission was different. It had no mandate to negotiate with the South African government, nor would that have been possible. Rather, its responsibility was to convince government and other political leaders to implement UN, OAU and WCC resolutions directed at the complete isolation of South Africa.

Developments inside the country gave evidence of continued deterioration. In February 1988, 17 non-violent anti-apartheid organizations were banned; by the end of the year that number had increased to 32. In August 1988 Khotso House, the headquarters of the SACC, was destroyed by a large bomb. Not long afterwards, Kanya House, headquarters of the Southern African Catholic Bishops Conference (SACBC), was also bombed and destroyed. The state of emergency was already 1000 days old. Thousands of people were still in detention, neither charged nor tried; hundreds were on hunger strike, demanding to be tried or released.

South African church leaders then called an emergency meeting in Geneva and explained anew the urgency of sending the ECPG on its mission.

In its report, the Sanctions Mission, as it was called, spoke about the "confused and hypocritical attitude to the use of violence in South Africa, one which amounted to a double standard; as well as an exaggeration of the reputed radicalism (the 'communist bogey') of groups opposed to apartheid, which in actuality expressed an ideological fear for the future of free market capitalism in South Africa". But, the Mission stated, "one impression stood out more than any other — behind the reluctance to take decisive action against apartheid in South Africa lay the power of persistent racism in the societies of Western Europe, North America and Japan."[27] The Mission found willingness to tighten sanctions in some countries, but all governments visited were opposed to comprehensive mandatory sanctions, arguing that these would not work. Meanwhile, the first signs of their effectiveness became clear when the South African minister of finance told parliament on 15 March 1989: "Every South African will have to make a sacrifice in the battle against an economic onslaught which is being organized against the country internationally."[28] Though the Sanctions Mission may have been only partially successful, its importance was that it represented the strong convictions of many churches and trade unions in South Africa and that it acted on their behalf in conveying the message of the last hour.

One further concrete sign of the international sanctions campaign received the endorsement of the WCC central committee in 1988: the boycott of the Shell Oil Company.[29] The central committee agreed that oil is the lifeblood of an industrial society and that in South Africa, with its military war machinery, the call for a boycott of this nature was another way of implementing its policy of isolation. But the WCC stressed in correspondence with Shell that Shell itself was not its enemy, much less its personnel or shareholders. The common enemy of humanity was apartheid. Other WCC campaigns included protests against the death penalty in political cases in South Africa. Also interventions were made to block the rescheduling of South Africa's debts.

In 1989 the SACC organized a small consultation in Harare on the legitimacy of the South African government. In an introduction to the meeting, Ninan Koshy, director of the WCC's Commission of the Churches on International Affairs (CCIA), said:

> The Constitution of South Africa does not contain even a rudimentary idea of the sovereignty of a people. The Constitution does not even claim to represent the majority of the people. It never went through any process to legitimate it. The voice of the people has not been heard. The Constitution of South Africa is illegitimate... The laws and institutions of government have to be for the good of the people at large. There is an implied social contract in Romans 13. When that social contract is broken, that contradicts the declared will of God.

Closely related to the issue of the illegitimacy of the regime was the question of capital punishment in South Africa and in particular the death penalty for politically motivated cases. South Africa had one of the highest rates of judicial executions in the world. According to figures from Amnesty International between 1978 and the end of 1987, the courts sentenced 1593 people to death. In 1987 alone, 187 people were hanged in Pretoria Central Prison. The state of emergency declared in 1986 rendered any expression of political opinion and mass mobilization against apartheid a punishable offence. Capital punishment became a means of political control.

The WCC, which in principle opposes the death penalty, launched an international campaign with other non-governmental organizations to exert as much pressure as possible on the regime to abolish the death penalty by addressing the peculiar circumstances of South Africa and the special way in which judicial execution was being used as part of political policy.

The goal in sight

The year 1990 finally brought the beginning of sweeping changes towards the end of apartheid rule. On 2 February, President F.W. de Klerk announced the government's intention to release political prisoners, unban political movements — in particular the ANC and the PAC — and negotiate a new constitutional dispensation for the country. On 11 February, Nelson Mandela came out of prison after 27 years of incarceration. Black South Africans exploded with a joy and excitement never before seen in the history of the country. World leaders paid tribute to Mandela for his courage and principles. In a speech to his supporters he reminded them of the words he spoke to the judge who sentenced him to life imprisonment in 1964: "I have cherished the ideal of a democratic and free society in which all persons live together in harmony and with equal opportunities." Early in June, Nelson Mandela and his wife Winnie, together with a large ANC delegation, visited the WCC headquarters in Geneva. To a packed hall he paid a warm tribute to the work of the WCC over the years in solidarity with the people of South Africa. It was a memorable and emotional event.

Successive events posed a challenge to some fundamental policy positions of the WCC. What did these events portend for South Africa? How would they affect the ministry of the churches in South Africa? What would be the WCC's future role? To try to answer such questions, PCR organized a consultative emergency meeting in Harare a few weeks after Mandela's release. It assessed and interpreted developments in order to see how these would affect WCC policy against apartheid. The meeting listened to voices from the churches in South Africa and to the views of the liberation movements. The need to maintain the international pressure against the system was felt to be essential in order to force the government to start meaningful negotiations as soon as possible. Frank Chikane, general secretary of the SACC, underlined the continued role for the international church community. The WCC had mainly worked through the SACC, but it realized the importance of widening its contacts with the Southern African Catholic Bishops

Conference (SACBC), the trade unions COSATU and NACTU and a number of grassroots organizations.

In November 1990, a national conference of church leaders in South Africa was held in Rustenburg, Transvaal, under the title "Towards a United Christian Witness in a Changing South Africa". The week-long meeting brought together not only the member churches of the SACC, but also the Dutch Reformed and Roman Catholic Churches and observers from the WCC and other ecumenical organizations.

At the meeting, prominent DRC theologians publicly confessed their complicity in the sin of apartheid. Indeed, all the white church leaders admitted that, at the very least, they had sinned by omission, by excessive impartiality. The meeting achieved a measure of reconciliation between the ruling Afrikaner establishment and the churches with a black majority. Given the South African context, the meeting was an historic as well as a political event. But the big question remained: were the churches willing to become instruments in the reconstruction of their country?

At Rustenburg Beyers Naudé, who had suffered so much over the years from the attitude of his own church (DRC), apologized to the WCC for the injustice done to it:

> My deep conviction [is] that an apology from the DRC is due to the WCC for the serious wrong which it did to this world ecumenical body in 1961. But an official apology is also due to the ecumenical movement throughout the world where the National Party propaganda deliberately made the WCC the scapegoat of its own anger at the resolutions adopted at Cottesloe. For decades, the Nationalist propaganda machine deliberately created and sustained a totally distorted image of the WCC and of its important ecumenical role. For the sake, not of the World Council, but of the DRC and its acceptance in the ecumenical fellowship, there is dire need for this church to state its sincere regret to the World Council for this unfortunate development. How easy it would be to say: "We're sorry. Forgive us."[30]

Already in 1986 the WCC executive committee had modified the WCC's earlier decision (1975) to discourage visits to South Africa. At its meeting in Norway in September 1990, on the recommendation of the PCR commission, it formulated a new travel policy for the WCC and its member churches, stating that "visits are considered a proper means of furthering the struggle against apartheid, by supporting and strengthening democratic forces within South Africa. However, they are to be undertaken in response to a specific invitation from member churches in South Africa, the SACC or from organizations recognized by the WCC as being representative of the struggle for liberation". But the homelands remained excluded from such visits. Member churches were also discouraged from "self-invitation" to South Africa.[31]

Thirty years after the DRC had left the WCC, it sent official observers to the Council's seventh assembly in Canberra in February 1991. This assembly was not as much preoccupied with southern Africa as previous assemblies had been, though the issue of racism in many other parts of the world, particularly the situation of the Aborigines in Australia, received considerable attention. However, the PCR did organize a small brain-storming meeting on the situation in South Africa during the assembly, which posed some critical questions about the churches' responsibility in the interim period preceding a post-apartheid society.

Apartheid and the struggle against it had fostered a "culture of violence", said a paper prepared for the meeting, quoting the observation by Frank Chikane that "the most tragic reflection of the war situation in which South Africa finds itself is that it faces the years to come with children who have been socialized to find violence completely acceptable and human life cheap".[32]

The present situation could not be understood without acknowledging that it was the result of the long and brutal tyranny of dehumanization by apartheid. And, the paper added, "the church must now actively involve itself in addressing and eliminating poverty, providing adequate health, welfare and educational facilities... Hitherto, part of the church has involved itself mainly in the political battle to dismantle apartheid. As rapid changes are taking place, the church needs to involve itself in the socio-economic situation, highlighting the problems by making a theological analysis."[33]

The assembly itself recognized in a statement on South Africa that "the liberation struggle, as well as boycotts, economic sanctions and other measures which have served to isolate South Africa from the world community of nations, have combined to produce a growing momentum for change. It is already becoming evident, however, that the next phase in the movement for a new, democratic and non-racial South Africa might yet prove to be the most difficult phase of all."[34] While many apartheid laws were being abolished, the discriminatory structures and practices which had created them remained intact. In particular, the government had made no commitment to a policy of fair and just redistribution of land.

An important moment came in October 1991, when WCC general secretary Emilio Castro visited South Africa at the invitation of the SACC. It was the first visit to the country by a WCC general secretary since 1970. Accompanied by several members of staff, Castro made pastoral visits to the member churches and the SACC. He also went to refugee centres and communities ravaged by incessant violence. There were many occasions of ecumenical mourning as well as rejoicing. Castro met President F.W. de Klerk as well as Nelson Mandela and other leaders of the ANC, PAC, the Azanian People's Organization (AZAPO) and the Inkatha Freedom Party, appealing to the leaders on all these occasions to do everything in their power to help end the violence in the country.

The visit ended in Cape Town with a jointly sponsored SACC-WCC consultation, "Towards an Ecumenical Agenda for a Changing South Africa", attended by church leaders from around the world. The "honeymoon" period after Mandela's release and the unbanning of the liberation movements in 1990 was over. Apartheid was not dead, the WCC delegation was told time and again when they met men, women and children living in squalor, but still with tremendous dignity, hoping for a future and asking why it had not come.

The consultation heard numerous reports of covert violence by unknown persons, the so-called "third force". It called for reconciliation between churches and between conflicting groups in the nation. And reconciliation, it said, included restitution of land and property. Without this, peace could not be achieved.

The meeting called for "an effective monitoring system" on violence, to be supervised by an international group with adequate powers to investigate, report and ensure appropriate action.[35] This appeal was strengthened in May 1992 at an SACC-sponsored Emergency Summit on Violence in which leading politicians and church people participated. In a memorandum to President de Klerk, the SACC urged the need to "recognize the value of an international monitoring mechanism of this violence". It was clear that the churches could perform a role which no other group could undertake — a role which could be made more credible by international participation. This was important because the SACC's own integrity had to be beyond question. It could not afford to be perceived as taking sides with any political group.

In South Africa there was a great deal expected of the WCC. Political movements and trade unions had emphasized the continuing role of the WCC at this critical stage, especially its possible contribution to monitoring the violence. The WCC, it was felt, could offer constructive criticism to the liberation movements, but above all it would have to support the churches in South Africa in their efforts to prepare for a new stage in the country's history.

This was the context when the Ecumenical Monitoring Programme in South Africa (EMPSA) started its work in September 1992. A joint venture of the SACC, SACBC and WCC, it was meant as a distinctive operation, yet working in close cooperation with similar UN, European Union, Commonwealth and OAU efforts to monitor violence, negotiations and the electoral process leading up to the first democratic elections based on universal franchise in 1994. Initially four ten-person teams were involved, from churches in Canada, Denmark, Finland, Germany, Kenya, the UK and the USA. In all, some 300 international monitors were to be deployed during the period October 1993 till July 1994. The WCC executive committee agreed in March 1993 to extend EMPSA's mandate for three months beyond the elections.

In September 1993, Nelson Mandela, addressing the UN Special Committee against Apartheid, officially called for the end of most sanctions against his country. The implications of this decision for the anti-apartheid movement worldwide, and not least for the churches and the WCC, were considerable. The WCC's longstanding policy of supporting sanctions was reviewed by its central committee meeting in Johannesburg in January 1994. Recognizing the need for translating the vision of a new South Africa into innovative and workable models, the SACC, SACBC, Institute for Contextual Theology (ICT) and Kagiso Trust, anticipating the end of sanctions, had convened a conference at Broederstroom in February 1992, entitled "Towards a Code of Investment-Ethics for South Africa's International Economic Relations". Following the meeting, the SACC and SABC created a Task Force on Economic Matters, composed of prominent South African theologians and economists.

These and other initiatives towards justice and peace by the churches in South Africa need the full commitment of the ecumenical movement. In particular the WCC's continued support at this crucial point in the history of the people of South Africa will be all important. It must not give up after all these years of intense involvement, now that the building blocks for a constitutional democracy have finally been put in place.

The preamble to South Africa's interim constitution adopted in November 1993 starts with these words:

> In humble submission to Almighty God, we the people of South Africa declare that whereas there is a need to create a new order in which all South Africans will be entitled to a common citizenship in a sovereign and democratic constitutional state...

That is only the beginning.

NOTES

[1] John Vincent, *The Race Race*, London, SCM, 1970, p.60.
[2] *Ibid.*, p.33.
[3] *WCC Central Committee Minutes*, Canterbury 1969, pp.143-44.
[4] *Ibid.*, pp.270-73.

⁵ See E.W. Anderson, *The Vulnerability of the Cape Route*, London, Foreign Affairs Research Institute, 1982 (this Institute was subsidized by the South African government in the 1970s).

⁶ C.F. Beyers Naudé, "The Parting of the Ways", *Pro Veritate*, 15 October 1970.

⁷ *WCC Central Committee Minutes*, Addis Ababa 1971, p.55.

⁸ *Ibid.*, p.247.

⁹ Ruth First, *The South African Connection: Western Investment in Apartheid*, London, Temple Smith, 1972.

¹⁰ *Violence, Non-Violence and the Struggle for Social Justice*, Geneva, WCC, 1973, p.16.

¹¹ *The WCC and Bank Loans to Apartheid*, WCC/PCR, 1977.

¹² *Racism in Theology and Theology against Racism*, Geneva, WCC, 1975, p.7.

¹³ *Ibid.*, p.8.

¹⁴ Quoted in *WCC Statements and Actions on Racism 1948-1979*, Geneva, WCC, 1980, pp.38-40.

¹⁵ Alexander Kirby, *South Africa's Bantustans: What Independence for the Transkei?* Geneva, WCC, 1976.

¹⁶ Derrick Knight, *Beyond the Pale: The Christian Political Fringe*, London, Kogan Page, 1981, p.81.

¹⁷ *Ibid.*, p.98.

¹⁸ *WCC Central Committee Minutes*, Geneva 1980, pp.70-71.

¹⁹ *Gathered for Life*, ed. David Gill, Geneva, WCC, 1983, pp.222-23.

²⁰ *Ibid.*, pp.196-97.

²¹ *Ibid.*, pp.152f.

²² James Mutambirwa, *Report on the WCC Harare Meeting*, WCC/PCR, 1985, pp.2-4.

²³ *WCC Executive Committee Minutes*, Reykjavik, September 1986, p.28.

²⁴ *The Churches' Search for Justice and Peace in Southern Africa*, report on meeting in Lusaka, Zambia, WCC/PCR, 1987, p.28.

²⁵ *Ibid.*

²⁶ Charles Villa-Vicencio, *Civil Disobedience and Beyond: Law, Resistance and Religion in South Africa*, Cape Town, 1990, pp.97, 136.

²⁷ James Mutambirwa, *South Africa: The Sanctions Mission Report of the Eminent Church Persons' Group,* Geneva, WCC, 1989, p.119.

²⁸ *International Herald Tribune*, 16 March 1989.

²⁹ *Shell Shock: The Churches and the Oil Embargo*, WCC/PCR, 1989.

³⁰ C.F. Beyers Naudé, "The Role of the Church in a Changing South Africa", in *The Road to Rustenburg: The Church Looking Forward to a New South Africa*, Cape Town, Struik Christian Books, 1991, p.227.

³¹ *WCC Executive Committee Minutes*, Granvollen, September 1990, p.33.

³² *Monitor*, Journal of the Human Rights Trust, December 1989, p.12.

³³ *Papers and Addresses for the Record*, WCC/PCR, 1990, pp.8-11.

³⁴ *Signs of the Spirit*, ed. Michael Kinnamon, Geneva, WCC, 1991, p.219.

³⁵ "From Cottesloe to Cape Town", *PCR Information*, No. 30, October 1991, p.104.

3

Political Involvement

ELISABETH ADLER

Footnotes can sometimes be very revealing. The introduction to the report of a 1964 ecumenical consultation on "Christian Practice and Desirable Action in Social Change in Southern Africa", carries one such footnote:

> There were members of the consultation who felt bound to dissociate themselves from any suggestion that the use of industrial disruption, the invoking of sanctions or other forms of international intervention, or the use of internal violence are permissible methods to secure social justice. Some members of the consultation were of the opinion that it is not the task of the church as an institution or organization to undertake to produce and to carry into effect specific economic and political solutions to human problems.[1]

This spans the whole spectrum — from criticism of certain methods used to achieve social and racial justice to reservations about the political involvement of churches in general — which was later to mark controversies around the Programme to Combat Racism. In the report itself such reservations are indeed nothing but a footnote. The consultation, held under the auspices of the Mindolo Ecumenical Foundation, the South African Institute of Race Relations and the World Council of Churches, was driven by the urgency of a situation in which the trend was moving from non-violence to violence. "Many are convinced that war has already begun."[2] What could Christians do in this situation? How could they resist injustice? The answer of the consultation was: by spiritual resistance, by legal political opposition, by civil disobedience and — only as the last resort after serious questioning of motives and consequences — by supporting the use of force.

The consultation did not question the need for political involvement. It clearly affirmed the churches' responsibility for justice in southern Africa. It reminded the churches of their prophetic task to discern evil, to resist it, to call the people of God to repentance and to create a climate for change of the present policy.

What the ecumenical movement together with the South African churches had to learn about political involvement was foreshadowed at Mindolo:

— The church is challenged by the situation.
— The church tries to decide how to respond to it.
— The church is divided about if and how it should get involved.
— The church finds theological and political reasons to remain neutral.
— The church discerns its own complicity.
— The church takes sides with the poor and the oppressed.

In the following pages I will show some of the controversies which the ecumenical movement encountered and some of the experiences and theological insights it gained by getting involved in politics in the struggle against the sin of racism and the heresy of apartheid. I do this in three parts. First, I ask if the church can be truly the church when it avoids political involvement. Second, I show how the church always exists in a specific socio-political context and often works in complicity with the existing structures. Third, I point to the ecumenical conviction that the church can be "the church for the world" only if it becomes the church of the poor and the oppressed.

Let the church be the church

"The task of the church is to convert the world, to Christianize men and women... and to leave politics aside," wrote Bishop A.C. Headlam, a leader of the Faith and Order movement, in 1945.[3] He was opposed to the foundation of a World Council of Churches which would make statements on political issues, as the Life and Work movement had done. The first assembly of the WCC — despite such warnings — declared that its mission was to bring the good news to the whole world and to speak to the powerful in the name of Christ on behalf of the poor and oppressed. Throughout the history of the ecumenical movement there have been other voices like Bishop Headlam's who have questioned the WCC's mandate in the realm of politics. These voices became more numerous and strident when the WCC inaugurated its Programme to Combat Racism. They have come from evangelical and conservative groups, from Orthodox and Lutheran theologians, from churches which directly or indirectly supported South Africa's apartheid policy. Their motives have been theological, political, psychological, ideological or a mixture of all of these.

White churches in South Africa used theological arguments to explain their refusal to support ecumenical statements and actions against apartheid. When the two Dutch Reformed churches withdrew from WCC membership after the Cottesloe consultation in 1960, one reason they gave was: "The consultation dealt with practical politics, on which the church should not express itself, unless some scriptural issue was involved."[4]

After the first grants to liberation movements were announced in 1970, the Dutch Reformed Church accused the WCC of having "forsaken the ministry of reconciliation and chosen the road of violence in its obsession with racial and political questions".[5]

The motive behind such objections was not only the church's conservative theology but also its theologizing of nationalism and the pressure exerted by the government. Prime Minister John Vorster wrote: "I go to church on Sunday and want to hear in the sermon nothing but Christ. I want to be a true Christian and hear about Christ not about politics." Eberhard Bethge, discussing the resistance of the Confessing Church in Nazi Germany and of the church in contemporary South Africa has shown how Vorster misused the *solus Christus* of the Confessing Church. Vorster wanted non-interference of the church in politics, while the Barmen declaration sought to guard the church against the interference of the Nazis in its message.[6]

There was also direct interference of the South African government in church affairs. The Eloff Commission investigation of the South African Council of Churches (1983-84) argued against the SACC's involvement in politics. The South African police submission to the commission insisted that churches should focus their concern on "personal salvation and conversion". It criticized the SACC on the grounds that it "does not involve itself in its primary area, and does not undertake... large-scale campaigns for money in overseas countries for converting non-Christians". And the commission itself recommended that the government should control the SACC's funds to ensure that they are used for "only truly spiritual purposes".

To recommend privatization of religion, in a country where religion has always been patriotic, was a way to reject the theologically based dissent and resistance of the SACC. In 1985, a group of some 150 South African theologians — both black and white — published a *Theological Comment on the Political Crisis in South Africa*, which became known worldwide by its popular title, the "Kairos document". Challenging the church to move "beyond a mere ambulance ministry to a ministry of involvement and participation", it declared:

> The church of Jesus Christ is not called to be a bastion of caution and moderation. The church should challenge, inspire and motivate people. It has a message of the cross that inspires us to make sacrifices for justice and liberation. It has a message of hope and confidence.[7]

Quite a different form of private religion and non-participation in politics was traditionally practised by evangelicals in South Africa. When the "total strategy" of the government was felt in every village and township and every sign of opposition was smashed by security forces, a group of "Concerned Evangelicals" came together to discuss the situation and their response to it. A year after the Kairos document they published a critique of their own theology and practice in a document called *Evangelical Witness in South Africa*, in order to liberate themselves for active participation in change. They said:

> Most evangelical groupings... consciously or unconsciously adhere to Luther's notion of the two kingdoms: the secular order and the spiritual order, which never mix. They argue that the church has nothing to say about this secular order or this earthly kingdom. [8]

The writers described the influence of theologies from abroad which had led people to accept the situation as God-given, using Romans 13 as an argument for maintaining the status quo. Positively, the document called for repentance and radical change.

> To try to extract some "spiritual life" from a political or economic life, in the name of "non-involvement" in politics, is dualism. This dualistic outlook on life is unscriptural. Life is a whole. A "born-again" Christian was not exempted from carrying a pass book, with its evil accompaniments! This is a political issue... We need to ask God to help us to see, hear and speak out. [9]

As in South Africa, affluent churches in the industrialized countries had more problems with critical involvement in politics and the PCR than did churches in the poorer countries. The richer churches did not deny that racism was contrary to the gospel. But they did not want the church to take sides in combatting racism. The church, they argued, should be above the parties in attempting to fulfil its genuine Christian task of reconciliation.

The controversy about the mandate of the church in the field of politics was at the same time a controversy about the WCC's mandate. Had the ecumenical movement lost its impartiality? Could the WCC fulfil a prophetic ministry and still keep the ecumenical fellowship together? In several reports to the central committee during his term as moderator, M.M. Thomas made passionate pleas for holding together the twofold task of the ecumenical movement. In 1972 in Utrecht he talked about "the priestly ministry of liberating reconciliation and the prophetic ministry of liberating conflict" and asked:

> How can we be at once messengers of peace in a world of strife, and messengers of strife in a world of false peace, that is, without breaking the

fellowship into messengers of peace and messengers of strife and without breaking the structure of the Council into instruments of charity and reconciliation on the one hand and instruments of provocation and of conflict for the sake of justice on the other?[10]

In 1973, he characterized politics as "an area of infinite possibilities for spiritual renewal" and rejected rigid compartmentalization of different fields of experience. Jesus Christ was in solidarity with the poor, he said, and the politics of liberation has to do with the order of Christ — not only with the order of necessity. "To my mind this after-politics Christ is only slightly different from after-death heaven."[11]

The slogan associated with the 1937 Life and Work conference in Oxford, "Let the church be the church", ought not to be misunderstood. This conference on "Church, Community and State", taking place during the Nazi period, did not call the churches to limit their scope to inner church matters, but to fulfil their ministry in all realms of life, thus relativizing all ideologies and powers.

The church in the world of politics

No matter how much the churches may shy away from political involvement and try to be neutral, they exist in particular social and political contexts. How much they are involved in racist structures from which they either benefit or suffer, how much they are themselves an active or passive factor in politics, was a lesson the ecumenical community has had to learn during the last 25 years.

The mandate of PCR called on churches "to confess their involvement in the perpetuation of racism". They were asked to become "agents for the radical restructuring of society".[12] The churches' complicity with racism was rooted in their history. They shared in the legitimization of colonialism and profited from it. Therefore the alienation was deep between churches of formerly colonized and colonizing, exploited and exploiting, racially oppressed and racially oppressive countries. A letter to member churches written by the WCC central committee in 1972 asked them to face up to the tensions rooted in centuries of injustice:

> We must re-examine ourselves in the knowledge of Christ's commitment to the poor and the outcast. Most difficult of all, we are becoming aware just how all-pervasive are the structures of racism and of economic oppression and thus how the struggle for justice inevitably divides us... We shall have to learn again and again to set our actions in social and political spheres in relation to the action of God in Christ.[13]

Without recognition of the deep divisions between churches — not only along denominational, but also along political lines — the ecumenical movement would be misguided in its work for the unity of the church. Ernst Lange, reflecting on the Faith and Order conference in Louvain in 1971, underlined the importance of the study project "The Unity of the Church and the Unity of Mankind". He called the PCR a test case for the whole experiment of looking at the unity of humanity as a Faith and Order issue. "What divides the world also divides the church."[14] The church as a part of the world is affected by racism. Racism becomes a challenge for the church, a challenge not only to its diaconal institutions, but to its faith. The church must begin the struggle against racism in its own house. Having become aware of its complicity in racism, it must end it.

Dietrich Bonhoeffer, recognizing that complicity with National Socialism was almost inevitable even for members of the Confessing Church, decided to join the resistance movement and to participate in a plot against Hitler. Eberhard Bethge, his friend and editor, reacting in 1986 to the South African Kairos document, reflected on Bonhoeffer's decision:

> The recognition of complicity and the breaking away from it seems to be for us today the decisive analytical criterion... Only with the triad of recognizing guilt, confessing guilt (individually and collectively) and carrying responsibility for it does liberation from complicity take place and create the conditions for forgiveness, reconciliation and healing.[15]

It was not only the white churches in South Africa but also the (white) churches from the North who had to change sides in order to disentangle themselves from complicity with racist structures. The refusal to resist oppressive systems and keep the church out of politics is itself a political option, the option for the status quo. In their reluctance to support the PCR or certain aspects of it, the churches have been blind to their own fears and the self-interest which made them opt for the status quo.

The Kairos document criticizes the theological defence of the status quo, which it calls "state theology":

> State theology is simply the theological justification of the status quo with its racism, capitalism and totalitarianism... State security becomes a more important concern than justice, and those who in the name of God work to change the unjust structures of society are branded as ungodly agitators and rebels... The state often admonishes church leaders to "preach the pure gospel" and not to "meddle in politics", while at the same time it indulges in its own political theology which claims God's approval for its use of violence in maintaining an unjust system of law and order.[16]

Critique of "state theology" by the Kairos theologians was more easily accepted by anti-apartheid churches inside and outside South Africa than their critique of "church theology". Here the churches' cherished principles of reconciliation and peace come under scrutiny:

> In our situation in South Africa today, it would be totally un-Christian to plead for reconciliation and peace before the present injustices have been removed... It is asking us to become accomplices in our own oppression... No reconciliation is possible in South Africa without justice, without the total dismantling of apartheid. [17]

The Kairos theologians spoke from inside the oppression. But even they felt the necessity to become liberated from complicity. The Concerned Evangelicals began their document with the recognition that their own churches "would be supporting the status quo instead of being the conscience of the state". They criticized the structural conformity, conservatism and anti-ecumenism of evangelical Christians and called them to be truly radical in fighting the sins of discrimination, oppression, exploitation and apartheid instead of fighting only a selected set of sins like adultery, drunkenness, hatred.

Neither in its 1986 document on *Church and Society* nor in the revised version of 1990 did the Dutch Reformed Church respond to the challenges of the Kairos theologians and the Concerned Evangelicals. As if these two documents of their fellow Christians did not exist, *Church and Society* says under the heading "The church is a reconciled fellowship": "The deeds of the church should be characterized by the spirit of reconciliation, peace and love...; churches will not promote confrontation, but will pray for one another." The 1990 version mentions the "prophetic function" of the church but gives no evidence of having listened to the prophetic voices of its sister churches. Instead, the DRC credits the ideal and policy of apartheid with "honest and noble intentions". It admits, however, that it had been too uncritical of its practice. "The church made the error of allowing forced separation and division of peoples to be considered a biblical imperative." Racism is called a sin, apartheid as such is not — only its "functioning" in such a way "that the largest part of the population of the country experienced it as an oppressive system". [18]

However, one month later, in November 1990, in Rustenburg, at the most representative consultation of South African churches ever held, a declaration was adopted which included a confession of guilt for legitimizing and supporting apartheid. The DRC delegation did not agree with a number of things in the declaration, which they said were "very one-sided", but the head of the delegation especially emphasized one sentence in the document: "On this issue all agree, namely the unequivocal rejection of apartheid." [19] In other words, complicity with racism and apartheid was finally rejected when the government itself began to dissolve the apartheid system.

The international political context of the time of these debates was the period of cold war, of polarization into two antagonistic camps, a time when injustices between North and South were overshadowed by the East-West confrontation. Therefore the churches' struggle against racism could easily be used as a tool by both communists and anti-communists. Because PCR was a programme for radical change, for the empowering of the oppressed, it was easy to label it "communist".

The WCC consultation in 1975 on "Racism in Theology — Theology against Racism" addressed this misconception:

> Anti-Marxism is often used to paralyze discussion of the struggles against structures of injustice in order to disqualify the exercise of political and social responsibilities... The increasing convergence of Christian and Marxist positions makes it all the more necessary to criticize openly and consistently the inherent dangers of new oppression, inherent in the Marxist ideological system. [20]

The Kairos document has a special paragraph on "the threat of communism":

> Anything that threatens the status quo is labelled "communist". Anyone who opposes the state and especially anyone who rejects its theology is simply dismissed as a "communist"... The state uses the label "communist" in an uncritical and unexamined way as its symbol of evil. [21]

The Concerned Evangelicals were outraged by white American evangelistic campaigns in South Africa which denounced what they called "communism" and "terrorism", while in fact preaching submissiveness to the oppressive apartheid system. [22]

The polarization was felt within the WCC itself. In debates on the Special Fund, disinvestment, white immigration and other issues related to the PCR, Eastern European church delegates were not very vocal. Western representatives often criticized the WCC's singling out of South Africa for statements and actions critical of government policies and supportive of oppressed people. Why did the WCC not do the same with the communist countries, where religious and ideological oppression took place and the people needed solidarity?

In fact it was the PCR-related debate on violence and non-violence which sparked the discussion on religious freedom and human rights in the socialist countries of Eastern Europe at the central committee meeting in 1973 and again in 1975 at the Nairobi assembly. At the central committee meeting, Alex Boraine of South Africa, commenting on the study document on *Violence, Non-violence and the Struggle for Social*

Justice, suggested that its not mentioning Eastern Europe as a region where Christians had to face pressure would be seen in South Africa as an argument against the WCC. Representatives from Eastern European churches had spoken very strongly against the inclusion of a paragraph on their countries. In Nairobi, a similar debate took place following the presentation of a document concerning the Helsinki agreements on security and cooperation in Europe.

It was difficult and sometimes painful for the ecumenical community not to be able to speak up with the same voice on injustices in different countries. The WCC did not follow a policy of "balanced" criticism of both the East and the West. The same form of political intervention was not necessarily useful in all situations. A contextual approach was needed and practised. The WCC spoke up against the apartheid system particularly because it was designed by Christians and enforced by a government which claimed to be Christian whereas communist governments never made such claims. Yet the learning process of the ecumenical community through the PCR affected all its members — including those from socialist countries. State interference in church life and the temptation for the church to assimilate to state policy were issues not only in South Africa; empowering the powerless, having a vision for the future society and feeling a need for political ethics were challenges not only for South African Christians.

The struggle has not yet ended. Racism continues to exist. Its roots are deeper and its dimensions larger than has often been realized. Ernst Lange understood already in 1972 what was at stake when he wrote:

> Combatting racism is a relatively harmless expression for the worldwide upheaval against the white destruction of the world, the institutionalized messianism of human groups with light skin, which tears the world apart. [23]

Even after state socialism has collapsed and the apartheid system has been dismantled, the process Lange described is still going on. And the church in the midst of it will have to respond.

The church for the world

"Oikoumene", the Greek word which means "the whole inhabited earth", has always inspired the ecumenical movement to understand its mandate as implying that the church is there for the whole inhabited earth. The themes of WCC assemblies have echoed this: Jesus Christ is the hope, the light, the life of the world. We expect the renewal of all things, of the whole creation. How can the church — following Christ — be the church for the world? The answer the ecumenical community has found is this: by being the church of the poor and oppressed. The experience of black Christians in South Africa has pointed in this direction. They have been teachers for the ecumenical community. As Desmond Tutu has written:

> I have not yet heard victims of oppression, those who live in deprived ghettoes or are uprooted and dumped in resettlement camps, or the banned and those detained without trial, accuse us of mixing religion with politics. If anything, they are concerned that the church is often not involved enough... For the oppressed the most vital part of the Christian gospel is its message of liberation..., liberation to be people who enjoy the glorious liberty of the children of God, which must include political empowerment to determine the shape of one's destiny. [24]

The process of learning has only begun among those who are not poor and not oppressed. Often "church for the world" is only used as a theologically correct phrase. The problem is that churches in the past and in the present have been "drifting away from the poor and powerless to the rich and mighty", as the report of the consultation on Racism in Theology pointed out. "This presents us with the duty of rescuing the legacy of suffering and resistance, of revolt and silent endurance, hidden in the history of the oppressed. This would give us a truer understanding of what is today being expressed in the theologies of black people."[25] The conclusion of the report is that the church needs to become again and again "the church of the suffering servant" who "reigns from the cross".

In Europe, North America, Australia and South Africa, churches have been part of the dominant culture which regulates all aspects of life — political, social and cultural. Being part of the dominant culture produces the feelings of superiority which perpetuate racism. Unless the church steps out of this hierarchical order of the dominant culture, it will not become the church of the suffering servant and the church of the poor and the oppressed. This is why the WCC in the mandate for the PCR called for a decisive ecumenical act of solidarity, which meant shifting to the other side, standing beside the suffering people:

> We call upon the churches to move beyond charity, grants and traditional programming to relevant and sacrificial action leading to new relationships of dignity and justice among all men and to become agents for the radical reconstruction of society. There can be no justice in our world without transfer of economic resources to undergird the redistribution of political power and to make cultural self-determination meaningful. In this transfer of resources a corporate act by the ecumenical fellowship of churches can provide a significant moral lead. [26]

If a similar call were to be formulated today it would probably be expressed in more moderate language and would alter the demand for radical change into a "more realistic" one. But the call for *metanoia*, for changing sides, is an even more urgent necessity for the church today, 25 years later. The churches' readiness and ability to become agents for the radical restructuring of society were overestimated, but they must be called to become participants in the suffering. The poor and oppressed — more articulate now — might soon use much stronger language and put the church aside as being always on the side of the rich and mighty.

Are the established churches in a position to move to the other side?

The Federation of Protestant Churches in East Germany, having lost the character of a folk church, found it not too difficult to express solidarity with the racially oppressed. Having moved away from a position of establishment, the churches were less privileged and therefore closer to the underprivileged. In evaluating the PCR in 1979 the federation strongly supported the extension of its mandate:

> Racism is today no less dangerous than five years ago; as the forces of liberation are growing, so also are the forces of resistance against change by those who profit from oppression... Not to listen to the voices of the powerful but to the voices of the oppressed and to place oneself on their side was an historic turn in the life of the WCC. Now it is decisive to show that the churches are not only standing occasionally on the side of the oppressed but are following Christ in principle and always. [27]

Does the church move and change only when it is forced to do so by circumstances? During the Nazi period, the folk church in Germany became a pseudo-church and those who insisted on the *solus Christus* assembled in the Confessing Church. In South Africa the history of the Confessing Church in Germany became an inspiration for those who rejected the biblical and theological justification of apartheid by white churches. During the 1960s it was especially Beyers Naudé who expressed the need for a confessing church in South Africa. In 1965 he published an article in *Pro Veritate* entitled "Die tyd vir 'n 'Belydende Kerk' is daa" ("The time for a confessing church has come"). What he had in mind was a movement within the churches which would be a prophetic voice in church and society. Such a movement was already in existence in the Christian Institute, of which he was director. In 1968 theologians from the Christian Institute and the SACC prepared a "Message to the People of South Africa", meant to be, like the Barmen declaration in Germany, a challenge to the conscience of every Christian in face of the heresy of apartheid and its unjust practices.

Besides the Confessing Church, the theology and personality of Dietrich Bonhoeffer influenced Beyers Naudé and his work. Eberhard Bethge visited South Africa in 1973 and lectured about the reception and interpretation of Bonhoeffer's theology. In an article on "Confessing

Church in South Africa?", he emphasized the differences between the two situations: in Germany in the 1930s Christians had to decide between the true and false church; in South Africa the challenge was to confess one body of Christ, the multi-racial church. [28] The Christian Institute and *Pro Veritate* became more "black", influenced by black liberation theology until they were banned in 1977.

In 1980, the black South African delegates at the consultation in Noordwijkerhout to review the PCR adopted a resolution concerning a black confessing church. "The churches to which we belong have conformed to patterns of racist society," it reads, and ends with the following paragraph:

> If after a period of twelve months there is no evidence of repentance shown in concrete action, the black Christians will have no alternative but to witness to the gospel of Jesus Christ by becoming a confessing church. [29]

They acted as a pressure group within the SACC, which continuously sensitized its member churches for non-collaboration and resistance against the apartheid system on the basis of their Christian faith.

When the government announced its "total strategy" against the enemies of apartheid from inside and outside the country, Wolfram Kistner, director of justice and reconciliation of the SACC, expressed the opinion that a situation had come in which Christians had no choice but to confess in the name of Christ their objection to the inhuman system. Apartheid represented a *status confessionis*, a situation on which the church had to take a stand. The Lutheran World Federation and the World Alliance of Reformed Churches declared at their assemblies, in Dar es Salaam (1977) and Ottawa (1982) respectively, that their member churches had to draw the consequences and reject apartheid unequivocally as heresy. Because the answers from the white Lutheran church and two white Reformed churches in South Africa were unsatisfactory, both world bodies declared the suspension of these churches.

Will rich churches ever become churches for and of the poor and oppressed? This is a question of life and death. "Today when you hear his voice, do not harden your hearts!" For Ernst Lange, being the church of the poor is the essence of the church:

> Jesus Christ as the rejected and broken one becomes the model of the wholeness of life. Therefore the presence of the marginalized in the church is not an act of ecclesiastical generosity; rather, how the marginal are central in the church and the weak strong in it is essential for the being of the church. Racism is not only sin but heresy, therefore a falsification of the gospel, a salvation-threatening perversion of the Christian truth, against which only excommunication can be used. [30]

Similarly, Frank Chikane, in an essay on "Doing Theology in a Situation of Conflict", speaks of involvement in the struggle for full humanity on the side of those dying of hunger and disease as indispensable: to do theology in a situation of conflict "involves being in detention with the victims of the system where one will be forced to ask realistic and concrete theological questions about God". This, he believes, demands a costly response: "priests should leave their mansions and live with the poor, weak and downtrodden to share in their struggles."[31]

Thus theology is not neutral but takes sides with the poor and oppressed. Theology as well as the church is "subversive" (and therefore regarded as dangerous). Both promote change, both are liberating forces.

NOTES

[1] *Christians and Race Relations in Southern Africa*, p.3.
[2] *Ibid.*, p.13.
[3] Quoted by Philip Potter, in *The Ecumenical Review*, XXXI, no. 2, April 1979.
[4] Peter Randall, *Not without Honour*, Johannesburg, Ravan Press, 1982, p.23.
[5] *DRC Newsletter*, July-August 1970.
[6] Eberhard Bethge, "Bekenntnis und Widerstand im Dritten Reich und Heute in Südafrika", in *Bekenntnis und Widerstand*, Hamburg, Evangelisches Missionswerk, 1985, p.501.
[7] *The Kairos Document: a Challenge to the Church*, 2d ed., Grand Rapids, Eerdmans, 1986, pp.29-30.
[8] *Evangelical Witness in South Africa*, Dobsonville, "Concerned Evangelicals", 1986, p.15.
[9] *Ibid.*, p.36.
[10] *The Ecumenical Review*, XXIV, no. 4, October 1972, p.409.
[11] *The Ecumenical Review*, XXV, no. 4, October 1973, p.409.
[12] *WCC Central Committee Minutes*, Geneva 1969, p.273.
[13] *The Ecumenical Review*, XXIV, no.4, October 1972, pp.475ff.
[14] Ernst Lange, *And Yet It Moves*, Geneva, WCC, 1978, p.99.
[15] E. Bethge, "Christen im Widerstand", in *KED Texte*, 40, Stuttgart, 1987, pp.263ff.
[16] *Op. cit.*, pp.3,6.
[17] *Ibid.*, p.2.
[18] *Church and Society*, Bloemfontein, 1991, paras 69-70, 279, 293, 284.
[19] Cf. *The Road to Rustenburg*, pp.92, 100.
[20] *Racism in Theology and Theology against Racism*, p.11.
[21] *Op. cit.*, p.7.
[22] *Op. cit.*, pp.30ff.
[23] Lange, *Die ökumenische Utopie*, Stuttgart, Kreuz Verlag, 1972, p.124.
[24] "Spirituality: Christian and African", in J. De Gruchy & C. Villa-Vicencio, eds, *Resistance and Hope*, Claremont, South Africa, David Philip, 1985, pp.162ff.
[25] *Op. cit.*, p.14.
[26] *WCC Central Committee Minutes*, Canterbury 1969, p.273.
[27] *Mitteilungsblatt des Bundes der Evangelischen Kirchen in der DDR*, 1974.
[28] *Study Encounter*, IX, no. 3, 1973, p.14.
[29] *Racism in South Africa*, report, Braamfontein, 1980, p.6.
[30] Lange, *Die ökumenische Utopie*, p.135.
[31] In de Gruchy & Villa-Vicencio, *op. cit.*, p.100.

4

Economic Strategies

An Evolving Prophetic Partnership between South African and US Churches

DONNA KATZIN

During the last half century, the international ecumenical movement and South African churches have been in a dynamic relationship in which the theology and experience of each has influenced and enriched the other. One of the most important components of that relationship has been the economy — as a matter of faith, an implement of liberation and a tool for transformation.

The economy as a matter of faith

The International Missionary Council (IMC) was one of the first ecumenical bodies to explore the challenges Christianity faces in a modern capitalist society. At its conference in Jerusalem in 1928, the Council underscored

1. The problems presented by the investment of capital in undeveloped areas and the necessity of securing that it take place on terms compatible with the welfare and progress of indigenous peoples.
2. The necessity, in developing the natural resources of such areas, both of protecting indigenous peoples and of securing the utilization of their resources for the services of the world as a whole, on terms compatible with such people's welfare.
3. The obligation resting on the governments of the economically more advanced countries to secure that economically less developed peoples are protected against economic and social injustice, and share fully and equitably in the fruits of economic progress...[1]

Ten years later, meeting in Tambaram, the IMC scrutinized its own economic practices in light of its mission:

A church which proclaims a gospel which transcends all distinctions of race, class and nation must take scrupulous care lest it deny that gospel by any

---

This paper has been written in consultation with Timothy Smith, executive director of the Interfaith Center on Corporate Responsibility.

policy or act savouring of racial, class or national arrogance. Here we wish to draw attention to the importance of the way in which church funds are invested.

The report cautioned that churches pursuing a lucrative income may be "tempted to invest their endowments or other trust funds in enterprises that are unworthy" or "not consistent with the things for which the churches stand". [2]

The contradiction noted by Tambaram — of making verbal declarations against racism while providing economic support to systems which establish and foster racial discrimination and oppression — has continued to be a theme within the World Council of Churches since its founding in 1948. The historical survey (Chapters 1-2) has shown that the economic realities of racism — both the poverty suffered by its victims and the power that wealth brings to its perpetrators — have always been in the forefront of the WCC's attention. From its beginnings in 1969 the PCR called for economic pressures to bring the apartheid system to an end. This process — including studies, public campaigns and boycotts of various kinds — proved to be a long and sometimes controversial one. In this chapter we shall look in particular at the role played in this initiative by the partnership between Christians in South Africa and the churches in the USA.

Economic strategies for liberation

Shortly after the 1960 Sharpeville massacre, Pretoria banned the country's democratic movements. South African churches, which were still allowed to operate legally, responded by raising their prophetic voice as standard bearers of the struggle against apartheid.

As South African religious leaders gave strength to the rising resistance within their own country, they also repeatedly called on the international community to exert maximum pressure on Pretoria. At a consultation convened by the National Council of Churches of Christ in the USA (NCC) and the United States Catholic Conference (USCC) in New York in 1977, Bishop Desmond Tutu challenged international partners:

> The West has a critical role to play to ensure the survival of all in our subcontinent, and you shouldn't abdicate your moral responsibility... You in the West have undergirded apartheid, injustice and oppression by your investments, by your use of your veto in South Africa's favour at the United Nations. You must decide where you want to be. [3]

In response the consultation recommended an intensifying effort to halt US corporate involvement in South Africa and urged support for legislation to deny tax credits to companies doing business there.

In 1981, Tutu, then general secretary of the South African Council of Churches (SACC), further exhorted the international community "for the sake of the children of all South Africans, black and white, for God's sake, for the sake of world peace", to take action and exert pressure on South Africa — "political pressures, diplomatic pressure and above all economic pressure".[4]

As the township resistance and rebellions flaring in 1984 and 1985 were met with Pretoria's harsh police crackdown and state of emergency, the South African churches faced their own kairos, the moment when God offers people a singular opportunity for repentance, conversion, new commitment and redirected action. In 1985, confronting a "moment of truth," the South African churches issued a seminal document which declared:

> Either we have full and equal justice for all or we don't. Prophetic theology therefore faces us with this fundamental choice and admits no compromises... Once we have made our choice, once we have taken sides, then we can begin to discuss the morality and effectiveness of means and strategies...
>
> This is our *kairos*. The structural inequality (political, social and economic) expressed in discriminatory laws, institutions and practices has led the people of South Africa into a virtual civil war and rebellion against tyranny.[5]

In 1985 the Southern African Catholic Bishops Conference (SACBC) called for the imposition of economic pressures to end apartheid and their intensification as other efforts failed to produce fundamental change, and the national conference of the SACC resolved:

> 1. to express our belief that disinvestment and similar economic pressures are now called for as a peaceful and effective means of putting pressure on the South African government to bring about the fundamental changes this country needs;
> 2. to ask our partner churches in other countries to continue with their efforts to identify and promote effective economic pressures to influence the situation in South Africa towards achieving justice and peace in this country and minimizing the violence of the conflict...[6]

The case for economic pressures

"We will win our freedom," Frank Chikane, general secretary of the SACC, said on more than one occasion. "The only question is how many more of us will have to die." In this context, economic pressures were viewed as a necessary complement to the struggle being waged at tremendous cost by South Africa's oppressed majority. Given the endemic violence of the apartheid state, the escalating cycle of rebellion and vicious repression and the ever-clearer potential for a massacre, civil war or both, international economic pressure was increasingly seen as South Africa's last hope for peaceful change.

Advocates of this strategy focused on the enormous contribution made by international banks, corporations and governments to the apartheid state. These included loans and other financial ties, trade and trade credits, direct investments, the reinvestment of profits and taxes paid to Pretoria by companies operating in South Africa, as well as the supply of strategic raw materials, products and advanced technology which South Africa was unable to produce competitively on its own. Moreover, these relationships cast a *de facto* vote of confidence in South Africa, and thus helped further to legitimize apartheid in international circles.

Although it was improbable that international measures would completely isolate the apartheid economy (given the acumen of South African and overseas "sanctions-busters" and the imperfect implementation of national and international laws), they did succeed in making goods and capital much harder to get. In the process they imposed an "apartheid premium" which absorbed an increasing sum of South African resources. These pressures also motivated South African decision-makers to channel thousands of millions of rands into projects (such as the production of synthetic fuel) which were aimed at bolstering the country's defences against sanctions but could never be economically competitive.

Together these strategies were designed to increase the cost of Pretoria's policies in order to make apartheid economically unsustainable and press the minority government to concede to majority rule. In 1987 the Evangelical Church in Germany commissioned the conservative Starnberger Institute to study the economic implications of sanctions against South Africa. The Institute concluded:

> Sanctions alone will not suffice to replace the apartheid regime with a more humane democratic alternative. However, economic sanctions can bring the apartheid regime to its knees economically and thus lend critical support to the front of democratic forces in South Africa.[7]

Religious advocates of economic strategies were frequently admonished for imposing increased suffering on the people they said they were trying to help. Their response, confirmed by the Starnberger analysis, was that apartheid's economic and political structures had imposed substantially more unemployment in recent years — and would probably continue to do so — than would be caused by the possible short-term effects of sanctions.

This position was supported in the US by data from the Investor Responsibility Research Center (IRRC). The IRRC reported in 1988 that since US companies then employed fewer than one percent of South

Africa's black workers, and only three percent of the employees of disinvesting companies lost their jobs, US corporate withdrawal affected fewer than .03 percent of black South African employees. [8]

The churches also offered a prophetic response to the charge that sanctions jeopardized the poor. Tutu declared:

> A clear message resounds in recent surveys in South Africa in which more than 70 percent of blacks supported sanctions against the government. Blacks are saying, "We are suffering already. To end it we will support sanctions, even if we have to take on additional suffering." I must ask, to whom is the international community willing to listen? To the victims and their spokesmen or to the perpetrators of apartheid and those who benefit from it? [9]

The ultimate goal of economic pressure was articulated with increasing clarity over time. At first, advocates simply called for an end to apartheid. Following the reforms announced by the De Klerk government in 1990, however, the South African churches found that changes were still "reversible", since the white minority retained the power to revoke them and to substitute new repressive measures. As a result, they appealed for continuing pressure. In June 1990 the national conference of the SACC clarified its understanding of what would constitute irreversible change:

> The dismantling of apartheid will be irreversible only when:
> i)   A constituent assembly is constituted;
> ii) Sovereign power is removed from the existing apartheid legislative structures and invested either in the constituent assembly or another agreed interim structure;
> iii) The white minority cannot legally reverse or veto the process of change through the present unrepresentative legislative structures.

Economic pressure had become an instrument for liberation.

US churches take up the challenge

International religious bodies responded in different ways to the South African churches' call for economic pressures. In this chapter, the US faith community serves as one of the numerous and diverse strands in the broad tapestry of multinational strategies to isolate the apartheid state.

Since the 1960s US churches had developed a unique partnership with the South African faith community. As they responded to their partners' call and heroic example, US churches followed their own prophetic path, bearing witness as part of their own civil rights movement. Martin Luther King Jr had urged the church to play a leading role in the struggle for freedom both at home and abroad, warning often that "those who oppose peaceful change make violent change inevitable".

From this perspective, the US religious community soon began to pursue a wide range of strategies to urge companies to end their business with apartheid South Africa. The churches started from the premise that, through their own investments and policies, they held a stake in the status quo both at home and in South Africa. In 1971 the Episcopal Church filed the first religious shareholder resolution for a vote at a corporate stockholder meeting when it submitted a proposal that General Motors withdraw from South Africa. During the two decades which followed, many of the 250 religious institutional investors working through the Interfaith Center on Corporate Responsibility (ICCR) coordinated similar resolutions to press more than a hundred US corporations to cut ties to South Africa.

Many churches which did not opt for shareholder activism chose instead to divest their portfolios by selling their stocks in companies with direct (and in some cases indirect) ties to South Africa. Their investments represented an important percentage of the $250 thousand million of US institutional holdings subjected to divestment policies in the 1980s.

The churches focused these strategies by campaigning for the withdrawal of corporations viewed as particularly strategic. Launched in 1985, the ICCR "Partners in Apartheid" campaign designated twelve US companies for special attention. One of the most strategic and dependent sectors of the South African economy was the computer industry. In 1971 the managing director of Burroughs Corporation (now UNISYS) in South Africa informed NCC researchers that the South African economy "would grind to a halt without access to the computer technology of the West. No bank could function; the government couldn't collect its money and couldn't account for it; business couldn't operate; payrolls couldn't be paid."[10]

The religious community directed a decade-long corporate campaign at IBM — the company which led the South African computer market since it installed its first machines there in 1960. In addition to shareholder resolutions, the tactics included post card campaigns, press conferences, prayer vigils and acts of public witness. Though these efforts helped to convince IBM to sell its South African operations in 1987, the company continued to distribute its computers in the country through its former subsidiary, and retained a lion's share of the computer market.

A second strategic sector was the petroleum industry. Shrouded in state secrecy, it sought to protect South Africa from the biggest chink in its natural armour: its absence of oil reserves. In keeping with the international oil embargo levied against South Africa first by the Arab League in 1973 and then by the United Nations, a large number of US Protestant denominations and Roman Catholic orders officially endorsed the Shell boycott (eventually launched in more than 17 countries) in 1986.

Although the boycott did not result in Shell's departure from South Africa, it had a demonstrable impact on the company. In 1987 ICCR received a copy of a confidential 264-page document written for Shell by Pagan International, the consulting firm it had hired to counter the boycott. While Shell did not carry out the strategies for all of its targeted constituencies, the company clearly viewed the religious community's participation in the boycott as of key importance. Shell's expensive campaign to neutralize the churches paid a curious compliment to the churches' influence. By the time the plan was intercepted many of the tactics aimed at the religious community had already been put in motion, though with minimal success.

The ICCR campaign directed at Mobil, the US oil company with the largest presence in South Africa, achieved its goal. Following a protracted campaign of tactics ranging from shareholder resolutions to civil disobedience, Mobil sold all its South African assets in 1989, agreeing to sever all ties to apartheid in five years.

Perhaps the most strategic sector of all was finance. Since the early 1970s South African religious leaders and anti-apartheid advocates around the world had underscored South Africa's dependence on foreign capital to build the apartheid state. As Pretoria sought to expand its infrastructure, fortify its military and protect itself from the increasing impact of sanctions, it borrowed heavily on international markets. Between 1972 and 1980 alone, more than 400 banks in 22 countries lent South Africa more than US$7000 million in publicly identified loans.[11]

Because of international pressure, banks around the world were forced to pass policies prohibiting loans to the South African government and its agencies. During the early 1980s many ended loans to the private sector as well. International banks, anxious about their escalating risks in the early 1980s, made increasingly short-term loans to South Africa, which they rolled over with mounting reluctance. In 1985, as the township rebellions and government repression spiralled, Chase Manhattan Bank dramatically refused to renew its loans as they came due, leading other banks to follow suit. This had a significant economic and political impact on South Africa, leaving the country with US$14 thousand million in short-term loans it could not repay, out of its total international debt of US$24 thousand million. The result was a South African moratorium on all short-term pay-backs, an agreement to reschedule the affected debt and mounting difficulty for South Africa in obtaining new financing.

US churches officially began their financial pressure campaign in the 1970s. In 1977 the NCC's governing board unanimously adopted a policy statement on southern Africa requesting the Council and its member denominations to withdraw their accounts from all banks making loans to South Africa. By 1987 US religious bodies had withdrawn more than US$125 million in accounts from Citibank alone.

The last US bank to withdraw its offices from South Africa, Citibank received continuing attention from the religious and anti-apartheid communities. Even after Citibank terminated its South African operations in 1988, religious investors and clients campaigned for Citibank and South Africa's other leading creditors, Manufacturers Hanover Trust and J.P. Morgan, to apply maximum pressure on the apartheid state. The churches advocated a stringent rescheduling agreement with South Africa, predicated on irreversible political change in that country, when its debt became due in 1990. They also pressed these and other banks to sever their day-to-day correspondent relationships with South African banks, thereby hampering the efficiency of South Africa's international commercial and financial transactions.

US religious bodies' diverse economic pressure campaigns converged in support for local and federal sanctions. In communities across the country, congregations, denominations and orders worked with other anti-apartheid advocates for local divestment, selective purchasing and contracting and banking ordinances. By 1992 such bills had become law in more than 160 cities, counties and states.

At the national level, led by faith-based organizations including the NCC, Washington Office on Africa, American Friends Service Committee and ICCR, US churches campaigned for legislation for comprehensive sanctions. Though the 1986 Comprehensive Anti-Apartheid Act (CAAA) was weaker than many advocates would have liked, it contained a number of powerful provisions including a ban on new investment in South Africa and a requirement that the US veto loans by the International Monetary Fund to any country "practising apartheid".

As US and South African churches shaped these strategies to end apartheid, they developed an intense and dynamic synergy. In the process they discovered that together they could use economic pressures to advance freedom by influencing the behaviour of multinational corporations and governments — thus bringing pressure successfully to bear on the apartheid state.

Economy as a tool for transformation
With the release of Nelson Mandela and unbanning of liberation movements and mass democratic organizations in February 1990, the faith community began to reconsider its role. As South Africa's major political organizations resumed their open leadership of the struggle for democracy, the churches began to anticipate a time when sanctions would

be lifted and a majority government would rule. In this context they began to focus on the task of redressing the legacy of apartheid and creating a just society.

In February 1991, the SACC, SACBC, Institute of Contextual Theology and Kagiso Trust convened an international conference in Broederstroom, South Africa, entitled "Towards a Code of Investment-Ethics for South Africa's International Economic Relations". The gathering posited the economy as a matter of faith and declared: "Our faith calls us to a prophetic and pastoral concern for the people of our country who have been disempowered and impoverished by the blatant and systemic economic distortions and imbalances created by apartheid."

The conference outlined the basic standards for conduct by which corporations investing in South Africa could help to reverse the historic oppressive patterns created by apartheid. It further called on the South African churches

> to urge the future government to formulate an investment policy which will promote holistic, democratic and sustainable development; [and] to urge and support the liberation and labour movements to produce a code of corporate conduct as a matter of urgency and establish a supervisory mechanism for its implementation. [12]

Following the meeting, the SACC and SACBC established an Ecumenical Task Force on Economic Matters composed of prominent South African theologians and economists. In a May 1993 document, adopted by the SACC's national executive committee, it explained:

> Investment projects as well as business ventures are unacceptable if they maintain the grim tradition of economic growth that benefits only a tiny, racially defined minority of the population...
>
> Even after the establishment of a democratic dispensation, the poor in South Africa will continue, for some period at least, to suffer from vast inequalities in income, wealth, living standards and power. In these circumstances, we cannot assume that management and investors will necessarily act in the interests of society as a whole. Rather, we must work to foster an ethical approach to the economy.
>
> Thus this statement of ethical standards for corporate responsibility is necessary.

This document built on the foundations laid at Broederstroom by spelling out more detailed guidelines for domestic and foreign businesses' relations with their workers, communities, consumers and the environment — as well as their potential contribution to national transformation and development.

The SACC and WCC convened an Ecumenical Conference on Ethical Investment in a Changing South Africa in June 1993 in Utrecht, the

Netherlands. The conference urged the SACC, in consultation with other "interested constituencies", to complete the development of an appropriate code to guide the conduct of both domestic and foreign corporations in South Africa. It added that the SACC should create an effective mechanism to monitor business behaviour as soon as possible, and called on ecumenical partners to provide the necessary financial and technical support.

The conference further recommended that churches around the world respond to an anticipated call by the South African democratic movement to lift sanctions by (1) discontinuing economic pressures (except for existing embargoes on strategic materials), (2) encouraging new investment and aid for all of southern Africa and (3) urging "business to share creatively and responsibly in the reconstruction process".

At its national conference the next month the SACC adopted a Code of Conduct for Business Operating in South Africa. These standards grew out of the churches' ongoing work with South African democratic and liberation movements, unions, communities and business, and with international partners. The code (printed in full as Appendix 1, p.127) reflects the religious community's prophetic pursuit of economic justice and its pastoral concern for disempowered and disenfranchised people. The code begins:

> The apartheid system has historically burdened South Africa with gross economic distortions, stagnation, secrecy, severe discrimination and natural devastation. It has deprived the country's workers, communities and environment of the fundamental rights written into international conventions and upheld in other countries.
>
> In order to reverse this crippling legacy and to improve the economic well-being of all South Africans, investment by both South African and multinational companies needs to be reshaped in the image of an equitable, democratic and life-enhancing society...
>
> This code... outlines ways in which business can play a constructive and creative role in partnership with workers, communities and other members of civil society, to lay the economic foundations for a stable and prosperous South Africa.
>
> While these standards are also expected to inform the policies of a democratically elected government, in the interim, they are designed to apply to companies operating in South Africa.

The call for responsible reinvestment marks both the culmination of decades of collaborative efforts and the birth of a new stage in the relationship between the South African and overseas ecumenical movements. As international partners have drawn inspiration and leadership from their South African counterparts, they in turn have given strength and direction to the emerging economic strategies to end apartheid. In the process their evolving prophetic partnership has created an important model for ecumenical work and international solidarity.

Today the reality of political democracy further challenges South African and international faith communities to participate in the process of transforming South Africa into a just society. It is a time of converging agendas, since South Africa is likely more and more to resemble US and European capitalist societies as it takes on the mantle of a Western style democracy. This probability has increased with the break-up of the Soviet Union and resulting dominance of the United States as the one surviving superpower. Thus today's churches confront parallel patterns and players at home and abroad which perpetuate institutionalized racism, historically rooted in economic and political oppression.

During this period, South African churches and their international partners have an opportunity to confront these challenges together. Will they succeed in holding their respective companies and governments accountable to new standards of economic justice? Will they be able to build a cooperative, equitable and empowering economy on the rubble of apartheid? Will they sustain the evolving ecumenical partnerships for a life-enhancing economy in a new South Africa — and beyond?

NOTES

[1] *The Jerusalem Meeting of the IMC*, Vol. V, "The Christian Mission in Relation to Industrial Problems", New York, International Missionary Council, 1928, pp.144-45.

[2] J. Merle Davis, ed., *The Economic Basis of the Church*, IMC Tambaram Report, London, Oxford University Press, 1939, p.600.

[3] *The Church and Southern Africa: Report on a Consultation*, New York, NCCCUSA, 1977, p.20.

[4] Quoted by Timothy Smith, "The Role of Foreign Banks in South Africa: Economic Support for Apartheid", United Nations General Assembly, A/CONF.107/7, 11 May 1981, p.7.

[5] Willis H. Logan, ed., *The Kairos Covenant: Standing with South African Christians*, New York, Friendship Press, 1988, p.30.

[6] Quoted in "US Churches Pledge Intensive Opposition to US Corporate Investment in Apartheid — Part Two", *The Corporate Examiner*, Vol. 14, No. 5, 1985, p.1.

[7] Cf. Donna Katzin, *Breaking the Ties: The Call for Corporate Withdrdawal from South Africa*, New York, ICCR, 1988, p.5.

[8] Jennifer Kibbe and David Hauck, *South Africa Review Service: Leaving South Africa: The Impact of US Corporate Disinvestment*, Washington, Investor Responsibility Research Center, 1988.

[9] Audrey Chapman, "Comprehensive Economic Sanctions Against Apartheid: Decisive Action for Freedom and Justice", *ICCR Brief*, Vol. 17, No. 3, 1988, p.3D.

[10] Richard Leonard, "Hardware, Software and Ingenuity for Apartheid: US Computer Companies in South Africa", *ICCR Brief*, Vol. 18, No. 1, 1989, p.3A.

[11] Smith, *loc. cit.*, p.1.

[12] Donna Katzin, "South African Churches Set Agenda for Economic Justice", *ICCR Brief*, Vol. 20, No. 10, 1991.

5

Mobilizing
the European Churches

DAVID HASLAM

When the Programme to Combat Racism was launched by the World Council of Churches in 1969 it took some time for the churches in most European countries to react. Certain radical Christian groups and anti-apartheid movements understood the importance of what had been initiated, and made their own response. Hence at the beginning of the 1970s a number of conversations took place among concerned individuals in countries such as the UK and the Netherlands — the countries with the strongest historical relationship to South Africa — and a little later in countries like Germany and Sweden. This led to the beginnings of an active response from Christians in Europe to the PCR.

The response was sharpened by the WCC's announcement of the first Special Fund grants in 1970. There had been little preparation in the churches for what quickly came to be regarded as an almost revolutionary initiative, and people known to be active in the ecumenical movement had a difficult time defending the grants. A few weeks after they were announced, the British Council of Churches (BCC) passed a lukewarm resolution which gave "general support" to the action and urged churches to make known the background information which had by that time become available from Geneva. But it also asked its Division of International Affairs to "gather material written from different points of view".

This emphasis on information and education became one of the crucial aspects of the PCR. By its action, particularly the granting of funds to groups and movements combating racism, the WCC compelled the churches in Europe and elsewhere to become aware of what was going on in southern Africa. Many churches were initially suspicious of the grants. Some openly opposed them, while welcoming the WCC's stated opposition to racism. Others gave cautious support. All however had to

---

Bert Boer and Karl-Heinz Dejung have also contributed to this paper.

do their homework and study the background to the grants. In this way the PCR proved to be an educational spur to the European churches.

This chapter focuses mainly on the accompanying campaign for financial disengagement from South Africa and the way in which the churches in Europe were gradually drawn into it. In hindsight, this emerges clearly as the most important dimension of the external struggle against apartheid. Most of the following examples are taken from the United Kingdom, which can be regarded as a kind of case-study of what was happening in Germany, Scandinavia, the Netherlands and elsewhere in Europe.

United Kingdom

When the PCR was launched, with its particular focus on apartheid, activists both inside and outside the UK churches quickly ascertained that some two-thirds of foreign investment in South Africa was British, although there were also important trade links with Germany and the United States. It was therefore decided that there was a particular role for British Christians to play in the external struggle against apartheid. In the early 1970s two church-based campaigns began in Britain: Christian Concern for Southern Africa (CCSA) and End Loans to South Africa (ELTSA).

Christian Concern for Southern Africa was begun by a group of individual Christians in 1972 to stimulate official church bodies to give more attention to British involvement in South Africa. In April 1973 the BCC instructed its Division of International Affairs to set up a unit to act for the churches on investment in South Africa. When this failed to obtain enough funding (largely because the Church of England refused to contribute), those who did want to work on this issue, including the Methodist Church and some missionary societies, decided to support the independent, newly formed CCSA.

During the 1970s, CCSA published useful reports on such major UK companies as the General Electric Company, Imperial Chemical Industries and Consolidated Goldfields, and on British banks. It urged them to end their expansion in southern Africa and to consider halting new investments or loans. It questioned whether it would really affect the apartheid system if companies fulfilled the Code of Conduct formulated in 1977 by the European Economic Community (EEC), although it supported the code's effort to ensure the setting up of black trade unions.

CCSA again drew attention to the weakness of the code of conduct approach in 1979, pointing out that there had been no assessment of the code's effectiveness by the British government's Department of Trade, and that many companies and indeed other European countries were ignoring it. The CCSA council decided that the implications of halting new investment and of economic disengagement should be explored. This move was partly due to the ongoing dialogue with the WCC, which had by this time come to the conclusion that disengagement was necessary.

During the 1980s CCSA's increasingly strong line in favour of disengagement from South Africa began to influence the British churches. It published a report entitled *Oil and Apartheid* in 1982, which highlighted the call of 24 church leaders for the oil companies to make reparations in Zimbabwe in recompense for their sanctions-busting. CCSA also helped to form the Ecumenical Investment Research and Information Service (EIRIS), which expanded from monitoring South African investment to researching ethical investment in many other spheres. However, CCSA always suffered from being a separate group trying to persuade the churches rather than an integral part of their official structures. The churches themselves continued to be cautious about participating fully in the struggle against apartheid.

End Loans to Southern Africa (ELTSA) was another campaign initiated largely by a group of individual Christians. Information had been obtained in 1973 from US sources that the Europe-American Banking Corporation (EABC) was making direct loans to the South African government. EABC included the Midland Bank (UK), AMRO (Netherlands) and Deutsche Bank (Germany). Campaigns developed in all three countries: ELTSA in Britain, *Betaald Antwoord* ("Prepaid Reply") in Holland and *Kein Geld für Apartheid* ("No Money for Apartheid") in Germany.

ELTSA began its campaign by holding a small protest demonstration outside the Midland Bank's annual general meeting and asking a church shareholder to raise a question within the meeting itself about loans to South Africa. The campaign progressed, through correspondence with the bank, to formulating in 1976 the first-ever resolution on a social issue presented to a British company, calling on the bank to cease making loans to the South African government. This received the backing of major church bodies, including the Methodist Church and the church commissioners of the Church of England. Since it was a properly proposed resolution, presented by the required number of shareholders, it had to be circulated to all those entitled to vote, together with a paper explaining the background to the issue. Thus it became a means of educating both the churches and the public about the situation in South Africa. Although the resolution achieved only six percent support, the Midland Bank made it clear within twelve months that it was no longer lending to the South African government.

ELTSA then focused attention on Barclays, a bank based in Britain but with a substantial share in the largest bank in South Africa. Together with the Anti-Apartheid Movement a vigorous boycott campaign developed, which received as much support from trade unions and students as from churches. Most churches had shares in Barclays at national level but were reluctant to use them to exert any pressure on the bank. Support came, however, from unexpected sources. The Caribbean Conference of Churches withdrew its accounts from Barclays and encouraged others in the Caribbean to do the same. Meanwhile, in the UK, a "shadow board of directors" created to monitor Barclays included among its members bishops, leading politicians, trade unionists and a film star. It published an "alternative annual report" each year, showing how the bank supported apartheid. A wide public, both within the church and beyond, was thus alerted to the South African apartheid policy and how it was being buttressed by British finance.

During the 1980s ELTSA campaigned increasingly at an international level. Its secretary appeared before the United Nations Special Committee Against Apartheid in 1979, and from this and similar occasions a network developed among those who were active in Europe, North America and the Caribbean, with support coming also from countries like Nigeria and Ghana. Many of these contacts were facilitated by church links. International days of action against banks and oil companies in particular proved effective, and received backing from the PCR.

Oil became the second most important campaigning area in the economic effort to undermine apartheid. Shell was thought to be the main company involved, and after the effectiveness of the resolution to the Midland Bank in 1976 ELTSA worked with others to bring a similar one to Shell's 1979 annual general meeting. An initiative was also undertaken at the annual general meeting of Royal Dutch, the other half of Shell. Over the next decade joint activity between Dutch and British church and anti-apartheid campaigners brought increasing pressure to bear on the giant company. The churches gave modest support to the Shell campaign and their representatives sought meetings with the Shell management, but they gave little support to the boycott itself.

During the 1980s Shell gradually reduced its business with South Africa. It was challenged particularly on the sale of oil and oil products to the military forces. In 1984 a report was produced jointly by CCSA, PCR and others, entitled *Fuelling Apartheid*, which told the story of sanctions-busting and suggested that, as in Rhodesia in the early 1970s, Shell could and should have known that its products were supporting racism.

Despite such evidence, it was not often possible to persuade churches as such in any European country to take effective action on the economic front. In the UK, for example, the church commissioners, who hold most of the large investments of the Church of England, refused either to sell their £22 million worth of Shell shares or to say publicly whether they were putting any serious pressure on the company.

Involving British churches

The BCC published in 1970 an important report, *Violence in Southern Africa: A Christian Assessment*. It described the current realities in the region, stating that white South Africa was fairly self-sufficient, that economic sanctions would take a long time to work and that the liberation movements had little likelihood of overthrowing the government. It did however suggest that Christians should show solidarity with those seeking fundamental change in South Africa, offer training and development support and begin to boycott firms with interests in South Africa.

This report laid the foundation for a special BCC assembly resolution regarding South Africa. By the following year the BCC was prepared to welcome the controversy provoked by the WCC's Special Fund, and urged contributions to it. It also encouraged the churches to develop their own education programmes.

The Methodist Church was the first to resolve, in its annual conference of 1971, to "examine the question of investment in southern Africa and to have its concern expressed at company meetings". This resolution was passed on to the church's central finance board. When the board's rather bland report came back to the conference two years later, it was rejected as inadequate. The conference welcomed the WCC decision to sell investments in companies helping to maintain apartheid and urged the Methodist Church to move out of such firms. In 1974 the Methodist Church supported the campaign against the Midland Bank's loans to South Africa and agreed to its own missionary society's giving support to the PCR.

The United Reformed Church (formed in 1971 by Congregational and Presbyterian churches in the UK) resolved in 1974 to ask its finance department to press for better conditions for black workers in firms operating in South Africa. The Baptist Union produced its own publicity on PCR. The Society of Friends issued a pamphlet stressing the importance of non-violent action for social change in South Africa. The Presbyterian Church in Ireland and the Salvation Army became outspoken opponents of the PCR and in particular of its Special Fund.

The most influential church in Britain is the Church of England. In July 1973 its general synod called on its Board of Social Responsibility to study the whole matter of investment in southern Africa; and in November a private motion was brought to the synod urging that no church money be invested in companies who disregarded their employees' interests. A more negative motion called on the WCC to reconsider its policy of disinvestment from South Africa. The next year the synod refused to support CCSA, and the following year reduced its grant to the WCC by a thousand pounds to express its disquiet over the policy of the PCR.

A 1973 BCC report on *Investment in Southern Africa* supported pressure on companies to improve their practices but indicated that this strategy was not likely to be ultimately successful, and that the option of withdrawal would probably become the most appropriate policy. This and other church reports, including one on *The World Council of Churches and Bank Loans to South Africa*, published by the PCR in 1977, led the way to a more far-reaching BCC report in 1979, entitled *Political Change in South Africa: Britain's Responsibility*. The assembly resolution accepting this declared its conviction that "progressive disengagement from the economy of South Africa" was now the appropriate approach for the churches. It commended to the government, the companies and the churches a series of steps which would lead gradually to a military, economic and oil embargo against South Africa. This report and resolution laid the foundation for the increased pressure brought to bear by the churches in Britain and in other European countries during the 1980s.

One of the first church actions to take place in the 1980s was the sale by the Roman Catholic archdiocese of Birmingham of shares in ten UK companies with involvement in South Africa. About the same time the BCC called a special conference to follow up its 1979 report and resolution. During the conference the Church of Scotland reported that it was opening conversations with three Scottish banks about loans to apartheid and investigating the involvement in South Africa of companies in which it held shares. The Society of Friends reported that they were discussing whether disinvestment was what they described as "a coercive strategy". The churches in Wales had taken no action. The Methodist and United Reformed churches both reported that they were engaged in dialogue with companies with interests in South Africa. The Church of England commissioners reiterated their position of being unable to avoid investment in such companies. They were using the EEC code of conduct to open up discussions on ways of improving the conditions of black employees. A policy of disengagement, they argued, would be "neither practicable nor right". Anglican missionary societies said they were unsure what they could do within the law, though the Society for the Propagation of the Gospel (SPG) was supporting the campaign to persuade Shell to stop supplying oil to South Africa.

In early 1981 the Church of England hosted two meetings with Leon Sullivan, a black Baptist minister from Philadelphia (and later a director of General Motors), who had drawn up his own principles for US investment in South Africa. These received some support from church financiers, though anti-apartheid activists expressed the belief that the principles would in the end have little effect.

Meanwhile the Anglican Board of Social Responsibility had been undertaking a review following the BCC's 1979 report. Its 1982 report, *Facing the Facts*, focused on the issue of economic disengagement. It reported on the meetings with Sullivan, but suggested that codes of conduct could not ensure fundamental change. The board urged the church and its financiers to press openly for disengagement, and argued that the British government should support the UN position. For the first time, it called for church support for certain dimensions of the work of anti-apartheid and liberation movements, and for a wide range of church and government action to create effective sanctions in sport, culture, trade, migration and investment.

The debate in the Church of England was revitalized in September 1985 by a report from Frank Field, a Member of Parliament who was also a member of synod. It detailed the result of a survey carried out on how the EEC Code of Conduct was being observed in 44 companies in South Africa, in each of which the church commissioners had investments of over a million pounds. It was noted that the commissioners had sold shares in the US company Carnation because of low pay to black workers. But the report also stated that many UK companies were paying similarly low wages or were refusing to provide the appropriate information.

In August 1985 South African Prime Minister P.W. Botha made a speech stating that South Africa was now "crossing the Rubicon", and there could be no turning back. The South African Council of Churches, sensing a kairos time of change, hurriedly invited a team from the British Council of Churches to visit South Africa and assess the nature of that change. The BCC team, after an intensive ten-day visit at the end of September, reported that "P.W. Botha has not yet come to his Rubicon, but the black people of South Africa have crossed theirs". The team cited a survey of 800 black South Africans, of whom 73 percent supported limited investment or none at all and 57 percent believed disinvestment would help to end apartheid. Their report called on the British churches to continue to scrutinize their investment practices and noted that proposals on targeted sanctions were to come before the next BCC assembly.

The British visit coincided with an announcement by international banks that they were declaring a moratorium on loans to South Africa and negotiating a repayment package with the government. It seemed they had succumbed to a combination of external boycott and moral pressure and were recognizing that things had to change internally in South Africa for the sake of its own long-term economic future.

In November 1985 SACC general secretary Beyers Naudé was invited to address the Church of England general synod. Courageously, he emphasized the need for sanctions and urged church financiers to disengage from "any institution which directly or indirectly supports the apartheid regime". He was received with a standing ovation.

In July 1986 the General Synod once again debated sanctions, encouraged by a Board of Social Responsibility report *Prisoners of Hope*, which suggested making contact with the African National Congress and other liberation movements and urged that the oil embargo should be made more effective. It concluded that black people in South Africa were stating that they were prepared to bear the cost of further sanctions and that pressure must be brought to bear on the South African government to begin talks with "the true representatives of the majority". After a detailed debate the synod resolved to call on the British government to impose effective sanctions against South Africa.

Christian anti-apartheid activists next kept a vigil outside the church commissioners' offices and launched a petition from Anglican clergy calling for further action on disinvestment. However, a private motion at the following synod requesting this of the church commissioners was rejected.

This period was typical of church response, particularly from those controlling ecclesiastical funds. The moral and political argument had finally been won, but it was difficult, at times almost impossible, to obtain any meaningful and costly action.

The Netherlands

After the launch of the PCR in 1969 a group of opinion leaders in the Netherlands came together and formed the working group known as "Prepaid Reply" (*Betaald Antwoord*). The very name expressed their eagerness to formulate an answer to the challenge of the Special Fund and to ask the churches to contribute to it.

It was clear from the beginning that the Special Fund would cause division in the churches. Those supporting it would be accused of aiding terrorism and communism and of fomenting opposition to white "civilization", law and order and even Christianity itself. Several pro-apartheid groups were formed, partly funded by money secretly given by the South African ministry of information. These groups began to slander those within the churches who dared to support the liberation struggle in Southern Africa, shamelessly appealing to overt or hidden racist attitudes.

This propaganda affected discussions in the churches' governing bodies and even undermined their actions.

Before the churches took an official stand — which, with some reluctance, they eventually did — Prepaid Reply took immediate action in appealing to them for financial support for the Special Fund. The small Remonstrant Brotherhood was the first to make a donation. The Netherlands Reformed Church (NHK) and the Reformed Churches in the Netherlands (GKN) followed with symbolic grants, despite heavy protest from many members and church officials. Subsequently, the synods decided to open special bank accounts for those congregations and members willing to give to the Special Fund, rather than making grants from general church funds.

From its first year Prepaid Reply publicized its fund-raising activities and raised substantial contributions to the Special Fund. Among the prominent Dutch people to contribute personally was Queen Juliana. A number of Roman Catholic monastic orders and congregations also became donors. From the mid-1970s until 1991 the Dutch government granted $250,000 annually to support the liberation movements in their responsibilities towards their many exiled compatriots.

The contributions to the Special Fund from Dutch churches and individuals have remained consistent to the present day, with Prepaid Reply continuing to draw their attention to possible new ways of supporting PCR following its relaunch in 1992.

But Prepaid Reply did not limit its activities to publicity and fund-raising. In vigorous cooperation with others such as Working Group Kairos, the Inter-Church Council for Peace (IKV) and the Council of Churches in the Netherlands, Prepaid Reply gave immediate support to the WCC resolutions on investments in southern Africa and emigration to South Africa, and developed strategies for bringing these concerns to churches, political movements, industry and banking. This close cooperation made it possible to build up a widespread awareness of the seriousness of the struggle against racism in its institutional form throughout southern Africa. The voices of prominent leaders of liberation movements and Christian organizations were frequently heard in Dutch churches.

On this basis Prepaid Reply acted both as catalyst for and conscience of the churches. It declared itself in favour of the 1972 resolution of the WCC central committee calling on companies to withdraw from South Africa and took steps to bring pressure to bear on selected companies, in particular Philips, Dutch Concrete, Bos Kalis and Shell.

After supportive decisions on disinvestment taken by the Dutch Council of Churches in 1975, the churches gradually acted on these recommendations. Representatives of churches joined members of action groups in delegations taking up discussions with companies. Thereafter, Prepaid Reply's role as initiator and catalyst was able to diminish.

In the second half of the 1970s specific attention was given to those banks which were still making loans to the South African government and its institutions responsible for arms production, electricity and oil. A combination of a consumer boycott against the leading Dutch banks (ABN, AMRO, NMB, RABO) with extensive correspondence between WCC general secretary Philip Potter and the banks brought them in 1978 to the point where they promised not to make any new loans to South Africa and not to extend the present loans when they expired. In the years following, Prepaid Reply discussed with the banks the question of putting pressure on Dutch companies still investing in South Africa by refusing to finance their activities. The banks would not agree to this, but the talks received considerable publicity and caused them some embarrassment.

Prepaid Reply also had an active team of educators working on a review of children's books to monitor traces of implicit or explicit racism. A dossier was prepared with materials and suggestions for authors, publishers and schools; and publishers were asked to withdraw or amend children's books and comics found to contain racist elements.

Federal Republic of Germany

When the WCC established the PCR in 1970, there were high hopes among some Christians in the Federal Republic that the Evangelical Church in Germany (EKD) would be particularly supportive. Through the Confessing Church of the 1930s, German Protestants had had the experience of confronting the criminal racism practised by the Nazi regime, and it thus seemed reasonable to expect a sense of solidarity with those combating racism in Southern Africa. On the other hand, there were close links — economic, political, cultural and ecclesiastical — between Germany and white South Africa and Namibia. The question was whether the German churches would try to avoid coming into conflict with the powerful interest groups within their own country and in their own ranks, or whether they would consider solidarity with the black majority in South Africa more important.

The WCC's action mobilized a broad grouping of people in Germany who organized themselves in numerous local, regional and national movements aiming to contribute to the realization of freedom and justice in southern Africa and to give their support to the actions recommended by the PCR. The experiences these groups had with the EKD and its regional churches (*Landeskirchen*) over the past twenty-five years have been contradictory. Although the churches readily associated themselves with the ecumenical confession of racism as sin, they had reservations about putting this theological insight into practices of the kind advocated by the WCC. They preferred to adopt what were officially called "multiple strategies".

This meant that until the late 1980s the German churches withheld official support for the aid given to liberation movements through the Special Fund of the PCR, though some individual churches did send contributions. Towards the end of the 1970s there had even been threats of the EKD's breaking off fellowship with the WCC so long as the latter continued to involve itself in what the EKD regarded as politically controversial questions.

The main area of controversy between those working in the action groups in Germany and the established churches of the EKD centred on the WCC's call for disinvestment and military sanctions. This debate highlighted the following considerations:

    a) the problem of the military and technological cooperation between Siemens and other German firms and Pretoria in the nuclear field;

    b) resistance to economic sanctions aimed at isolating white South Africa; as early as 1972 the EKD formulated a "complementary strategy" to that of the WCC, setting up a dialogue with German industry and favouring a "code of conduct" for German subsidiary companies in South Africa.

    c) refusal by the EKD until the late 1980s to challenge the major German banks to withdraw credit facilities from South Africa. The first breakthrough for the *Kein Geld für Apartheid* movement came about through a campaign organized around the Kirchentag, which had been sponsored by some of the banks.

While the action movements sought to force the demise of apartheid by ending collaboration between German economic powers and white racism, German churches emphasized the evolutionary effect of economic progress, which they hoped would eventually break the chains of apartheid.

It must be acknowledged that over the past 25 years German Christians, through their financial weight, have made a considerable contribution to work for justice and reconciliation in South Africa, partly in the context of PCR and partly in the framework of bilateral relationships with churches in South Africa and Namibia. Yet there was little solidarity between the official churches and the campaigns undertaken by the action groups. One reason for this was that German banks and businesses saw themselves as playing a role in the struggle to overcome apartheid and persuaded the churches to support them in this, even though the primary basis of their policy was the interests of the German economy rather than the experience of the liberation movements and the churches in South Africa.

In addition, there were theological grounds on which the German churches warned repeatedly against too much solidarity with people engaged in liberation struggles. They feared that over-identification could lead the church to give itself uncritically to the service of political objectives and systems, thereby compromising the gospel. This warning against "too much solidarity" was for the EKD itself a result of the struggle of the Confessing Church against National Socialism in the 1930s and 1940s. The action movements were aware of this legacy, and they also had painfully to learn that solidarity must always be "critical solidarity". But they felt that the theological insights gained in the struggle against the Nazis could not be simply applied to the struggle of the oppressed in South Africa lest the churches failed to respond to the suffering cry of the black majority there.

Scandinavia

In *Sweden* there was no immediate reaction to the launch of PCR. But after the 1972 WCC central committee resolution recommending withdrawal of investment in South Africa, the Swedish Ecumenical Council decided its international committee should look into Swedish investment in South Africa. Since the four main political parties in Sweden were represented in this committee, there was important political input into the debate. By April 1973 the committee was suggesting more support for change-oriented groups within Southern Africa and a survey of business and church involvement there.

A questionnaire was drafted for companies, and discussions took place with the trade unions and the Federation of Swedish Industries. As a result of the survey and other information, the Ecumenical Council decided in March 1974 to recommend to Swedish companies operating in South Africa that they improve black wages and working conditions and draw up an ethical code. The council also decided to be represented at company meetings, to urge Christians and church bodies to examine their investment in such companies and to remind the government that ultimately it was responsible for companies' behaviour. This went some way towards meeting the requests of the WCC resolution, though it did not fulfil them entirely.

The Ecumenical Council followed up its initiative with companies, political parties, the government and mission agencies. Some companies reacted negatively, but in March 1975 Archbishop Sundby, who chaired the Ecumenical Council, attended the annual general meeting of ASEA, the largest Swedish company in South Africa, and raised questions about its involvement there. Representatives of the Ecumenical Council also went to other shareholders' meetings that year.

This laid the foundation for an active programme of PCR support by the Swedish churches. No Swedish banks were ever implicated in loans to South Africa, so the banking campaign did not function there except on international days of action, when Swedish Christians joined in the challenge to German, British and Dutch banks. The Ecumenical Council kept up its pressure on Swedish companies remaining in South Africa.

In *Denmark*, the Ecumenical Council, which includes both the state Lutheran Church and the small minority churches, decided in autumn 1971 to respond to the launch of PCR by establishing a special account to receive donations. It encouraged church members to inform themselves about racism, but it did not endorse the PCR. When PCR was launched, the inter-church aid agency Danchurchaid decided at first to make a grant of US$5000, but later changed its mind, in order "to keep aid activities and politics separate".

In 1972 some Christians at the Aarhus Ecumenical Centre, in the absence of any official response, established a Churches' Race Programme, which focused on education for pastors and youth leaders and set up a research project into Denmark's economic relations with South Africa. In mid-1973 it issued a list of questions to the East Asiatic Company (EAC), the largest Danish investor in South Africa, and formed a shareholders' group. Later it formulated a two-year policy of pressure on Danish companies to ensure a radical improvement in black wages and conditions. An investigatory committee would then report on what had been achieved, and, if the results were not satisfactory, Danish companies should begin withdrawing from South Africa.

Norway did not see much action initially on PCR. However, church concern in all the Nordic countries bore fruit in 1978 when all five countries issued a programme of action prohibiting new investment in South Africa and restricting production. Early in the 1980s there was again joint action by the Scandinavian countries in supporting the Krugerrand boycott and also boycotting Shell. Nordic countries abstained from voting on the 1982 $1100 million IMF loan to the South African government. Later in the 1980s the main issue for Norway was the revelation that Norwegian-based oil tankers had been helping to breach the oil embargo against South Africa, and some vigorous campaigning took place against the companies, and involving government, in which the churches took some part.

Other European countries

A good deal of activity took place in *Switzerland*, partly because the WCC headquarters is there and partly because of the heavy involvement of Swiss banks in support of the apartheid regime. However, it was particularly difficult to mobilize the churches to take action on this issue. The Swiss Protestant Church Federation (FEPS) has no authority over the individual cantonal churches. Discussion was stimulated among the churches in late 1973 when the WCC produced its list of companies involved in South Africa. FEPS sent the churches a memorandum describing the PCR recommendations on disinvestment but did not itself urge any particular action.

Some of the cantonal churches gave their support to the PCR. The Geneva Church opened an account for members' donations. Churches in St Gall, Zurich and Thurgau gave financial assistance to the programme, but not to the Special Fund. FEPS began to help facilitate dialogue between churches, business people and action groups.

Three Swiss banks — the Swiss Banking Corporation (SBS), Crédit Suisse and the Union Bank of Switzerland (UBS) — became key targets in the international banking campaign. The churches seemed to find this something of an embarrassment and did not give a great deal of support to the anti-apartheid movements who were heading up the action. Some individual Christians participated in the boycott campaigns and in pickets outside the central offices of the banks in different cities.

The other main campaign which developed in the 1980s was against the heavy purchases of South African gold by the Swiss banks. Again, there was hardly any church action on this issue, although the sale of gold was South Africa's economic lifeline after the banks issued their loans moratorium in 1985.

In *France* the Protestant churches are small, and only four of the seven are WCC members. The French Protestant Federation (FPF) was therefore unable to take a strong position on the PCR. When the list of companies operating in South Africa was published in 1973, 58 French firms were on the list. This caused some reaction from the companies but little from the churches. The FPF did not react when the WCC passed its 1974 decision to withdraw from the six banks in the EABC, which included Société générale from France.

The Protestant churches in *Belgium* are also small, and did not take any stand in the first few years of PCR's existence. The main church claimed to have no investments in South Africa and no accounts with Société Générale (Belgium), another EABC member. The Protestant federation, however, was influenced by the PCR's position and began to encourage church-supported aid projects for liberation movements. The Roman Catholic Church's Justice and Peace Commission gave support to the WCC's position, and continued to be active in anti-apartheid activity through the 1970s and 1980s.

Overall, during the twenty years of campaigning in Western Europe for one form or another of financial sanctions against South Africa, those who were active in the movements and also trying to mobilize the churches came to see that boycotts and direct action can prove effective in the long run. The churches were not entirely inactive, but many opportunities for prophetic action were lost.

At root, the problem seems to have been a theological one. There are those who see the most important activity of the Christian churches to be bringing good news to the poor and setting at liberty those who are oppressed. There are others who seem to see their prime role as protecting the ecclesiastical institution, both in terms of public respectability and of financial resources. They feel they must resist anything that puts either of these at risk. The struggle against apartheid exposed the differences between these two approaches. But it is to be hoped that all parties learned something from the debate.

6

Tumultuous Response
The Voices of the South African Churches

BARNEY PITYANA

South Africa in the 1970s was in the stranglehold of Prime Minister B.J. Vorster's National Party regime. Vorster was riding the crest of a wave of popularity. Many white church people may have voted for the opposition, but they thanked God for the National Party in government. Church teaching was falling on deaf ears. The controversy sparked by the grants from the Special Fund of the WCC's Programme to Combat Racism could not have been more unwelcome for the churches. It opened the way for the government to take tough action against them.

Such was the prevailing atmosphere that the churches were caught in a whirlpool of anti-communist rhetoric and white nationalist fervour. The church, led as it was by white conservatives, abandoned its autonomy in some essential respects. Church theology proved inadequate to confront the state-sanctioned apostasy. These matters are now being discussed in a radically changed climate. What this changed climate does is to open the window to a period of the churches' history which has not benefited from rigorous examination.

This chapter will concentrate on activities within the eight WCC member churches in South Africa as well as the South African Council of Churches, the national ecumenical body with which all these churches were also affiliated. The SACC is in turn an affiliated council of the WCC. It is difficult to find a collective terminology for these churches. They are often called the English-speaking churches, but that does not take account of the Baptist Union, which consistently took a more reactionary line and was not even a member of the ecumenical body. The Roman Catholic Church, on the other hand, though only an observer member of the SACC, was fully associated with the social concerns of the ecumenical movement in its rejection of apartheid. By far the majority of the members of these churches, being black, did not conduct their ordinary church life through the medium of English. To refer to them as mission churches is also a misnomer, because that term is used in the

South African context to refer to the churches founded by mission societies among black communities as, for example, the Bantu Presbyterian Church (Church of Scotland), and the Tsonga Presbyterian Church (Swiss Protestant Mission). To call them mainline churches would be to bestow a status which all churches ought to share in common. For that reason they will be referred to here simply as WCC member churches.

The political context

The beginning of the 1970s was marked by an increasingly confident government of South Africa. Vorster had come into power with a fierce reputation as an advocate of "law and order". As Minister of "Justice" he steered legislation through parliament which gave extraordinary powers to the police and introduced the banning order mechanism to silence and control political opponents at home. Despite the repression, there was a high growth rate in the economy. One could say that South Africans never had it so good. And yet disparities between the rich and poor, black and white, remained stark.

The other leg of South African policy was an aggressive foreign policy, which went variously by the names of "detente" or the "outward-looking" policy. A confident pariah state could venture out of its isolation at the first signs of a thaw. South Africa was looking for friends. African states were divided in their attitude towards the apartheid giant further south. A much-publicized 1970 state visit by Malawi's President H. Kamuzu Banda, first of its kind by an African head of state, was later followed by the establishment of diplomatic relations with Malawi, the first African envoys to be accredited to Pretoria. Soon thereafter Cote d'Ivoire's President Felix Houphouët-Boigny signalled a change of policy in his relationship with the apartheid regime.

Vorster and his defence minister P.W. Botha embarked on another strategy, that of despatching troops to the neighbouring states. Vorster explained this policy of "hot pursuit" in these terms:

We shall fight terrorism not only in our own country but also in any other country in Africa where the government requests us to do so. If plans were laid against South Africa on such a large scale, and if the proposed build-up of terrorist forces becomes a reality, and if terrorists were to invade South Africa with the permission of those countries, we shall resist them. If they take flight we shall chase them, and we shall do so right into those countries from which they came. [1]

Such sabre-rattling served two purposes. It created an atmosphere of war-preparedness at a time when the white community felt vulnerable. According to state propaganda, communist terrorists were massing on the borders of the country and posed a threat to security. Second, it offered a justification for the anti-communist ideology. Both these strategies helped to rally white people around the policies of the regime. Further, government policy was designed to divide international opinion on South Africa. Parading South Africa as a bulwark against the expansionist communist ideology in the region ensured sympathy from the Western alliance.

Within South Africa, Vorster had come to believe that internal revolt had been crushed. The ANC and PAC, operating from exile, could be contained. Their underground activities within the country did not cause much concern except when it was considered necessary to exaggerate the threat for political purposes. The Bantustan policy appeared to be gaining acceptance. Bantustan leaders like Chiefs K.D. Matanzima and Gatsha Buthelezi were being portrayed by the liberal press as the voices of pragmatic opposition to apartheid.

What opposition there was to the policies of the Vorster regime came from the liberal front, diverse though that was. It ranged from the conservative accommodation of the South African Institute of Race Relations to the persistent exposés of injustice championed by the only opposition Member of Parliament, Helen Suzman, and English-language newspapers like the *Rand Daily Mail*. Some English academic institutions, led by the National Union of South African Students (NUSAS), together with Christian organizations like the Christian Institute and the University Christian Movement, tried to position themselves to the left of this front. A climate of fear and apprehension enveloped the country. Black liberative voices were conspicuous by their silence.

The emergence of the Black Consciousness Movement was to change all that. From among the oppressed, spokespersons came to the fore with an uncompromising message not dissimilar to that of the banned liberation organizations. The leaders imprisoned on Robben Island and in exile began to speak through hitherto unheard voices. The legitimacy of the struggle for liberation under the leadership of the oppressed was re-established.

The church in the 1970s

The world conference on Church and Society in Geneva in 1966, often characterized as a watershed in ecumenical social ethics, left an indelible mark on the ecumenical movement in South Africa as well. Two South African representatives were present: Bishop Bill Burnett, then general secretary of the Christian Council, and C.F. Beyers Naudé, director of the Christian Institute. During the course of 1967 they organized regional conferences in the major centres in South Africa to consider the findings of the Geneva conference. The church was thus made aware of the developments in ecumenical social thought and was challenged about the implications of these for South Africa. The South African Council of Churches (as the Christian Council was known after 1968) and the Christian Institute co-sponsored a national consultation on church and society in Johannesburg in February 1968. It affirmed the need for the churches to work for change in society, though in the circumstances of the time, the church, while maintaining its protests against the excesses of apartheid, never questioned the authority of the state.

The Message to the People of South Africa drafted by a theological commission and adopted by the SACC national conference in 1968 stated that the doctrine of separation was a "false faith, a novel gospel". The thinking then prevailing among white liberal Christians can be judged from a comment by a member of the SACC staff, Wolfram Kistner. He wrote that the dilemma of the sponsors of *The Message* was that if separate development were a false gospel, it had to be asked what alternative there was which would be acceptable to the churches. [2]

It is significant that even in this context the will of the majority of the people of South Africa and certainly of the oppressed was not considered to be a sufficient barometer for Christian reflection. On such a basis the two organizations co-sponsored the Study Project on Christianity in Apartheid Society (SPROCAS), designed to investigate the causes and effects of racism and to make proposals for an alternative society — this without regard to the fact that a succession of African leaders had projected a vision for a new South Africa, as if the Freedom Charter (1955) did not articulate expressly enough the vision of a new society, as if Albert Luthuli and Nelson Mandela had spoken in vain. Steve Biko, in a characteristically pointed remark, stated that the SPROCAS commissions were bound to fail because "they [were] looking for an alternative acceptable to the white people". [3]

It must be noted that the leadership of the member churches at that time was almost solidly white. Alphaeus H. Zulu was the first African to be consecrated bishop in the Church of the Province of Southern Africa (Anglican). Among the non-episcopal churches, Seth Mokitimi was the first African to be president of the Methodist Conference. The United Congregational Church of Southern Africa (UCCSA) had a majority black membership, and on many occasions this was evident in the positions which that church took. For most other churches, however, black participation was subordinate to white control. Many blacks in the churches were not identifying with the liberation forces or were thoroughly intimidated by an oppressive regime. Voices of liberation within the churches were muted and isolated.

Without the voice of the oppressed, and with the prophetic voices kept in check and marginalized, the church spoke the word of the conservative establishment. As it was in the political arena so also in the church: the white liberals were speaking for the oppressed. The oppressed remained a silent and invisible majority.

The South African churches and the WCC

All the evidence suggests that the relationship between the World Council of Churches and the representatives of the South African member churches became critical once the WCC turned its attention to South Africa. The positions taken at the Geneva conference in 1966 made the South Africans very uncomfortable about the direction then espoused by the WCC. They could detect a radical shift which did not augur well for the relations between them.

Burnett, representing the SACC, voiced his dissent from the sentiments expressed in the recommendations on the elimination of racism at the Uppsala assembly (1968), arguing that many of the statements implied support for violence. To the recommendations of the 1969 Notting Hill consultation that the WCC establish a programme to combat racism, the SACC once again raised objections, concerning the politics of the consultation, its understanding of racism, the apparent sanctioning of a resort to violence and the effectiveness of the proposed measures. The SACC response, approved by its executive on 6 August 1969, was apologetic in tone. Against the policy of sanctions, it counselled that corporations could not be compelled to do what they were not allowed to do by law; and that the WCC would not be allowed to carry out its policies in South Africa. While calling for a clear definition of racism, the intention was to deflect attention away from white racism by emphasizing racism between and among the racially oppressed groups in South Africa. The SACC statement called tribalism a form of racism, saying that "truth requires that we acknowledge unequivocally that racism is not confined to white persons..."

The idealism of the liberation forces was questioned: "even the best revolutionary intentions have a way of creating or institutionalizing new injustices that may never have been in the minds of their protagonists." By such a device, the churches were refusing to pay attention to the WCC's most pressing concern: the prevalence and growth of racism worldwide, and especially in South Africa.

Reactions to the grants

To say that the Special Fund grants announced by the WCC executive committee on 3 September 1970 "caused an emotional tide of reaction", as SACC general secretary John Rees put it, is an understatement. A better description would be that the announcement unleashed an avalanche of anger from the white establishment both in the church and in politics. It may be hard to understand why there was such a strong reaction, especially if one remembers that the Dutch Reformed member churches had already withdrawn from the WCC following the Cottesloe consultation under pressure from the Verwoerd government. The remaining member churches were known to be taking an enlightened view on the race question and apartheid in particular. Yet in South Africa in general the WCC was not held in much regard as a credible world Christian organization.

Of the amounts allocated from the Special Fund to liberation movements in Africa, a mere $10,000 was given to the Albert Luthuli Memorial Fund. The rest went to southern African liberation groups in Angola, Mozambique and Rhodesia. Why should such emotion be aroused when no South African liberation group received any funds directly? The grants were a logical consequence of the establishment of the Special Fund. No one should have been surprised. It would seem that this righteous indignation was orchestrated for political purposes as part of the renewed nationalism then sweeping the country.

The objections were however couched in ethical and theological terms. At one level there was the complaint that the South African partners were not informed in advance so that they could explain to their members the WCC's motivation for the grants. In reality this would not have changed anything. Church leaders would not have wished to be associated with the WCC action for fear of a backlash at home. It was politically expedient to plead ignorance, even though SACC general secretary John Rees and the only South African representative on the PCR commission, Alex Boraine of the Methodist Church, were both aware of the impending decision. They did nothing about it.

From the WCC's point of view it was logical to exclude the South African churches from this decision-making process altogether, either as a way of protecting them from the consequences back home or because they could not be trusted to assist in the understanding of this policy. The WCC had also come to understand that the church in South Africa did not represent the aspirations of the oppressed majority in the country. A radical shift was then underway from the institutional church to the church of the oppressed in those matters where the church could not or would not act. In the oppressive climate of those days, full disclosure of intentions and strategies was not advisable. The problem of communication between Geneva and South Africa is thus not surprising.

Rees told the WCC central committee meeting in Addis Ababa in 1971 that the South African churches objected to the churches' identification with organizations whose intention was to "change the social order in South Africa by the use of force". The truth was that SWAPO wanted South Africa to end its colonial occupation of Namibia, and the MPLA and Frelimo were fighting against colonial domination in Angola and Mozambique respectively. The Luthuli Foundation was established to promote the peace credentials of the late Chief Albert Luthuli following his award of the Nobel Peace Prize. Funds were to be used for scholarships for South African exiles. The critical issue turned on the question of violence. Is it theologically justifiable for the churches to support organizations whose purpose and intention is to overthrow the political order by means of violence?

There is no doubt that the response of the South African churches was orchestrated by the Vorster regime. The prime minister told the white-minority parliament:

> If they do not decide to dissociate themselves from this organization I would be neglecting my duty if I did not take action against them, if I allowed more money to be collected in South Africa for transmission to that organization, if I allowed churches which... remain members to send representatives to conferences of that body..., if I failed to take action against clergymen who allow pamphlets... to be distributed in their churches. [4]

While the general assembly of the Presbyterian Church was sitting in Cape Town, their leaders had dinner with Vorster, during which the prime minister pressed his case for withdrawal of membership from the WCC. Seen from within the confines of apartheid South Africa, it seemed as though the WCC had turned its whole attention on the situation in that country. It was not realized that the Council was addressing the vast global dimension of the problem of racism and racial discrimination, while recognizing that South Africa presented the most critical challenge to the Christian conscience of the world.

In January 1971 leaders of the WCC member churches in South Africa were granted an audience with Vorster. There was general agreement that the grants could not be justified. The only point of difference was whether the South African member churches were prepared to leave the world body as a result. The churches sought assurances that the government would allow a meeting with representatives of the WCC to discuss the grants. In the course of this apparently congenial discussion, one of the church leaders explained that a meeting was required in order to have a "confrontation" with the WCC over its grants. Vorster insisted from then onwards that the purpose of meeting with the WCC was to have a confrontation. The Vorster government was pushing the churches to withdraw their WCC membership in the same way Hendrik Verwoerd had pushed the Dutch Reformed member churches to the ultimate break in their relations with the WCC in 1960 after Cottesloe. The strategy was to maximize the demands, extract concessions from the church representatives and then sustain the pressure.

The churches played by Vorster's rules. They were set to resist calls for withdrawal from membership but allowed themselves to be manipulated in the process. The SACC was not sufficiently mindful of the overall thrust of the government strategy. By asking to see the prime minister and seeking assurances about a church meeting in South Africa, the church conceded the right of the government to interfere in matters of church life and responsibility. This attitude emboldened Vorster to insist on an agenda of "confrontation" with the WCC. Later, he refused to guarantee visas for the international delegation and eventually dictated that the "confrontation" should take place at Jan Smuts International Airport.

Some church leaders were anxious to be seen as patriotic. Leslie Stradling, an expatriate British missionary serving as Anglican bishop of Johannesburg, immediately reacted by saying that he could not justify support for "subversive movements which stand for violence and violent attacks on law and order." These were all buzzwords of patriotic South Africa. It is arguable that such sentiments were at variance with the spirit of *The Message to the People of South Africa* adopted by the churches in 1968. In referring to freedom fighters as "subversives" and entrusting the maintenance of "law and order" to the regime, Stradling was in effect accepting the legitimacy of the apartheid regime. Such a view of the situation echoed that of the Vorster government and the Dutch Reformed Church.

J.S. Gericke, moderator of the Dutch Reformed general synod, denounced the WCC's decision as "one of the most atrocious offences that the Christian churches can commit against the Word of God". The official statement of the DRC revealed an interesting motivation for its objections. It noted that the WCC had failed to support anti-communist organizations in Eastern Europe and that "terrorist bodies armed with Chinese and Russian weapons committed atrocities against South Africa".

The reaction of the other churches was more measured, though indignant in tone. The Presbyterian Church was the first to vote in its general assembly. By a vote of 75-57 it dissociated itself from the decision of the WCC, suspended its financial contribution but, by implication, refused to withdraw its membership of the WCC. A feature of its resolution was its effort to project a stance of neutrality and balance.

It stated that "it is generally no part of the Christian task to align the church with nationalist forces of any race" and it warned against identifying the church with white or black nationalisms. The assembly saw the need to insert into the resolution its "dissent from the violence inherent in the racial policies of the South African government".

The UCCSA affirmed its commitment to membership of the WCC and resolved to continue its financial contributions to WCC. However, it added that it "abhorred and rejected violence and terror as means to political change".

The Methodist Church maintained what had by then become a litany of condemnation of violence for political ends. However, it voted to retain its membership of the WCC, though it suspended its financial contributions. The Methodist Church raised strongly the matter of accountability, arguing that it was dishonest of the WCC to say that the Special Fund grants were given "without control as to the manner in which they are spent... as a commitment of the Programme to Combat Racism to the causes the organizations themselves are fighting for", whereas general WCC policy for grants required accountability and reports on the use of the funds.

The (Anglican) Church of the Province of South Africa, while dissociating itself from the WCC's action on the grants, resolved to retain membership of the world body. The CPSA acknowledged that the action was a condemnation of the racial policies of South Africa and confessed the failure of the church to be an effectual witness against injustice and inequality in South Africa. The CPSA criticized the WCC's decision theologically on the questionable grounds that it had failed to distinguish the circumstances under which the church considered it to be justifiable to take up arms and had abandoned its reconciling role in society.

The theological and ethical rationale for a programme of study and action for the elimination of racism had in fact been set out by both the Uppsala assembly and the Notting Hill consultation. Uppsala stated that racism was a threat to peace. The Notting Hill consultation put its understanding of reconciliation in these terms:

> The church is charged with the task of reconciliation. And if it is to take that ministry seriously, then it must attack racism significantly — at its origin, as well as the symptoms. Therefore, the church must be willing to be not only an institution of love but also an institution of action.

Regarding the ethics of violence, the WCC proceeded from the basis that where racism persists, violence and conflict are inevitable. The task is to support those who are the victims of racism and struggle for justice and liberation. The question of the morality of support for groups engaged

in acts of armed resistance is one which the WCC did not address directly
at this stage. No judgement was made as to the appropriateness of the
resort by oppressed groups to arms nor was there any explicit theological
justification of violence. But there was a commitment to solidarity and
common action to eliminate racism and oppression.

Theological analysis
    The reaction of the South African churches to the grants from the PCR
Special Fund raises a number of ethical questions about the theological
and ethical rationale for their attitude.
    a) Church-state relations. It might be thought that this issue would
have brought relations between the apartheid state and the churches to
their lowest ebb. The churches had consistently criticized apartheid and
the gross violations of human rights inherent in the application of
apartheid laws. Prominent church leaders had action taken against them
for their prophetic witness. The Anglican dean of Johannesburg, Gonville
ffrench-Beytagh, had to suffer the ordeal of a long trial for handling funds
to help the victims of apartheid. Two expatriate Anglican priests based in
Stellenbosch were unceremoniously deported because one of them,
Robert Mercer, had called for a balanced discussion of the issues that the
grants raised. Banning orders, deportations and refusal of work permits
for missionary workers were all the stock-in-trade of the government's
action against the churches.
    The church had scant reason to pander to the regime. But it did. It did
so because some held the view that Christians had a duty to obey the state.
Many failed to understand that the acts of repression then prevalent
entrenched the illegitimacy that had tainted the South African state from
its conception in 1910. The truth is that many white Christians strongly
supported the Vorster regime and were fearful of a democratic government led by the black majority. And so their young men accepted
conscription into the national service. Those church people against whom
action was taken were suspect. Yet churches resisted calls to withdraw
chaplains from the South African Defence Force. The campaign against
compulsory conscription received lukewarm support. There was a fervour
of patriotism among white Christians. All this raised questions about
idolatry and the new gospel that the *Message* warned against. Church
leaders, being white, understood only the sentiments of white Christians.
    Uneasy though the relationship between church and state was, the
power of the state was such that church leaders felt they had to walk the
tightrope of neutrality and moderation. This excessive moderation could
be detected in the failure to analyze political events thoroughly in order to
discover precisely whom they served.

The Methodist Church was obsessed with two ideas. The first was that the WCC analysis no longer held true in the region because white racism was no longer a simple factor. The examples were cited of black participation in the ill-fated Rhodesia-Zimbabwe government of Methodist bishop Abel Muzorewa and in Namibia/South West Africa. But the church documents failed to examine whether such blacks represented the opinions of the oppressed majority. In any event, such mechanisms did not signal a serious effort to change. Blacks were being coopted in order to maintain white minority control. Second, the Methodists failed to understand that the basis of giving the grants without any strings attached was a theology of sharing which expresses a solidarity based on trust and partnership — a theology subsequently developed by the Ecumenical Sharing of Resources discussion culminating in the El Escorial consultation (1986).

b) Theological method. Where it is the dominant and privileged group who articulate the theology, they simply enunciate the theology of the comfortable and the privileged. While "state theology", which Vorster spelled out with the help of the Dutch Reformed Church, was rejected by the churches, yet "church theology" in effect affirmed state theology.[5] The approach was not theological reflection drawn from experience but dogma imposed upon the believers.

The theology of non-violence and reconciliation sounded hollow when viewed against the churches' *de facto* recognition of an oppressive system. The church's silence or inaction in the face of the racial atrocities perpetrated in the name of apartheid betrayed its bias. Lacking the experience of the oppressed, the church did not appreciate what Jean-Paul Sartre meant when he said: "Our victims know us by their scars and by their chains, and it is this that makes their evidence irrefutable."

Even when the church purported to be neutral, it was taking sides for the maintenance of the status quo by the tried and true policy of protest without resistance. Charles Villa-Vicencio summarizes the contradictions within the English churches thus:

Captive to the dominant ideas of the dominant class and trapped within a theology of moderation and submission to the existing order, they have at best submitted to those within and without their own ranks who contended... that it was not their "proper function" to show solidarity with those who suffer if they resort to armed struggle, nor to lend theological recognition to those whose goal it is to "combat racism" in a manner in which their Christian consciences may dictate.[6]

c) The problem of selectivity. The South African churches sought to divert attention from the essential issues raised by the PCR with the defensive argument that the WCC should direct its actions to the repression prevalent in communist states. South Africa, it was claimed, was an avowedly Christian country resisting the communist onslaught. It was not appreciated that this ideological framework was not likely to change the attitude of a world Christian body like the WCC. For that reason it was easy to dismiss the WCC as a communist front.

It may be true that the WCC did not always pay sufficient attention to the situation behind the Iron Curtain, but it does not follow that less attention should have been paid to South Africa. The argument that where there is moral inconsistency, the status quo must be maintained is the ethics of criminality. Some wished merely to expound theory but when theory was applied to practice, they balked at the prospect. The diversionary theory points to innumerable situations of human rights violations the world over as a way of saying "why pick on us?" — as if that justifies the condition of inhumanity and injustice.

Because the question of continued WCC membership caused tensions within the Methodist Church, their conference authorized a study of the WCC and the ecumenical movement. In the subsequent report by Methodist theologians David Bandey and Donald Cragg, there was a defensive, even apologetic treatment of the relationship between the Methodist Church and the WCC. Particular criticism was reserved for the Programme to Combat Racism and its Special Fund. The booklet is closely argued and the objections of the Methodist Church are spelled out in detail.

d) The loud silence of the black voice. In the situation of the 1970s the representative voice of the oppressed had been silenced by exile and imprisonment. Bantustan puppets were discredited. Blacks were insignificantly represented in church leadership. In a repressive climate many black church people were wary of exposing themselves.

Among those black church people who were different was Bishop Alphaeus Zulu. His remarks were always measured, charitable and circumspect. He was one of the presidents of the WCC at the time of the announcement of the Special Fund grants. In his response to the announcement Bishop Zulu bemoaned the fact that there was no consultation with the South African member churches. As it turned out, he could not attend the crucial Arnoldshain meeting of the WCC executive committee where the decision was taken. Had he been there, he would have been aware of the sentiments behind the grants. Bishop Zulu's true feelings were however plainly stated in the T.B. Davie Memorial Lecture on academic freedom at the University of Cape Town in 1972, at a time when controversy about the grants was still raging in South Africa. He said:

And then, as everybody knows, the phenomenon of guerrilla warfare has become the standard method of fighting. It is taking place currently on our borders. Several African nations are committed to supporting the effort of the guerrillas against the whites of South Africa... The declared reason for this struggle is to give the black South Africans a freedom they honestly do not enjoy. Very few whites in this country are committed to non-violence and there is no reason why there should be any more commitment among blacks.

Anglican Archbishop Robert Selby Taylor, while condemning the decision of the WCC, drew attention to the fact that a state of violence already existed in the country. "We must not underestimate," he argued in his presidential charge to the 1970 synod, "the intelligence or knowledge or the Christian charity of those who were responsible for framing the resolutions to which we object. They know a great deal about what is happening in South Africa, and they see so much evidence of force and violence. They judge that a state of violence already exists, and they believe that we are being hypocritical when we condemn these in others..."

Another voice challenging and strengthening the resolve of the churches could be detected from the statement of the ecumenical students' organization, the University Christian Movement. While not justifying the WCC grants, the UCM drew attention to the inconsistent and hypocritical position of those who condemned them while remaining silent about other manifestations of violence in society. It questioned the motives of those who were silent when large amounts were being spent on arms and taxpayers' money was being used to send troops to Rhodesia.

Attention has already been drawn to the simplicity and superficiality of the churches' statements on reconciliation. Not only had the WCC's understanding of reconciliation been spelled out in the Notting Hill statement and by the central committee in Canterbury and Addis Ababa. More seriously, the churches had done nothing to bring about reconciliation in South Africa. Instead, they were on the side of the status quo, gullible to the extent that they appropriated the regime's language of "terrorists" and "law and order".

e) Towards a renewed understanding of the church. At the heart of the concern and hurt felt by the South African churches was the weakening of the ecumenical bond between member churches and the WCC. It was argued that there was a tendency in WCC circles to distrust the church representatives from South Africa.

What the WCC was signalling was that the church in South Africa needed to rediscover itself, to take seriously the voice of its black members and to extend its pastoral concern to those outside its walls, including the guerrilla fighters and refugees. The church had to become aware of the church beyond its own confines. Such a step would lead to a new ecclesiology for the South African church, which would take account of the hurt of the majority of the oppressed and powerless people of South Africa. The South African church should not merely be perceived in the light of the comfortable and dominant minority.

Following a visit to Lusaka in 1974, John Rees was magnanimous enough to confess how moved he was by the testimony of South Africans in exile. They told of their efforts to maintain Christian life in their military camps, including the training of Methodist lay preachers. He discovered that there were real Christians among the freedom fighters who shared the same confession as Christians at home. They were fully aware as Christians that they were responsible to God for their actions; and far from glorifying war, they bemoaned that it had become necessary to eliminate apartheid. Rees came to realize that the church of South Africa is not simply the church gathered in the comfortable pews of the suburbs but that base ecclesial communities functioned among the freedom fighters.

The WCC has struggled with the theological meaning of this ecclesiology from below in its own life. A network of grassroots movements converges around particular concerns. From time to time, the tension between the authority of the canonical churches and this network of groups surfaces. Not unlike the influential base ecclesial movements of the Latin American church, South Africa also has these base communities which have become as full a manifestation of the church as any institutional expression of it. The church in South Africa was being forced to recognize novel ways of being the church.

Lessons learned

Archbishop Robert Selby Taylor, then also president of the SACC, warned that the churches "must take positive action which will make it abundantly clear that we are not prepared to accept inequalities based on race". The churches undertook some self-examination. They all confessed their failure to act resolutely against racism and apartheid in both church and society. Rees expressed this feeling succinctly:

> If the only positive result of the WCC decision has been to make us acutely aware of the discriminatory society in which we live and to challenge the church as to where it stands, it has achieved a great deal.

One way in which South African churches demonstrated that they had listened to the messages from Geneva was the debate in the 1974 national conference of the SACC on conscientious objection. This acknowledged the tensions among Christians, black and white, because many had families and friends serving on both sides of the conflict. And so a programme of assistance and pastoral care to South African refugees was mooted.

Another result of the soul-searching in the South African churches was the SACC's establishment of an ecumenical Division on Justice and Reconciliation. In agreeing to it, the churches stated that this was one of the positive results of the WCC action. The programme investigated the structures and practices of injustice and oppression in South African society. It also supported the victims of apartheid through the dependents' conference, monitoring political trials, paying for the studies of prisoners, helping their families and continuing to support those who were released from prison and could not find employment.

The watershed

The year 1976 was a watershed in South African politics. It was the year when black students in Soweto rose in rebellion against the system of Bantu education, sought to undermine in various ways the structures of apartheid and defied the forces of oppression. These events sparked a variety of responses from the apartheid regime. At the social level, schemes to improve living conditions in black townships were undertaken through the Urban Foundation, so that new and better quality housing was provided which would attract the black middle classes. Restrictions on admission of black pupils to white private schools were eased. Later, Africans were to be allowed 99-year leases on their properties, and the Wiehan Report allowed registration of black trade unions. New constitutional devices were also set in place like the granting of "independence" to homelands. The policy of the government, then, was to consolidate its apartheid policies both in the Bantustans and in the urban areas. At the same time, it began tentatively to allow trade unions among black workers and improved housing and schools in black areas.

On the other hand, the South African economy was showing signs of strain. This was due in part to the international oil crisis but also to the impact of the economic boycotts sparked anew by the Soweto uprising. Unemployment was rising steadily. Yet the regime was engaged in a destructive and expensive war effort in Angola and in destabilization against its neighbours.

Despite all this, the government's own actions undermined its reform processes. Violence was becoming endemic, police were shooting protesters at will and detention without trial was a ready resort to contain resistance. So a new political response was devised. "Total strategy" was the answer to what was perceived as the "total onslaught" by communists and other enemies of South Africa at home and abroad. The power of the state was increased by 1979, centralizing all state functions in small committees. This served to marginalize parliament and increased authoritarian powers. Then a parallel system of government came into being — the National Security Management System (NSMS), which provided for a network of security committees operating at all levels of society and engaged in all aspects of social organization.

By the mid-1980s the NSMS had become the effective instrument of government. The state of emergency was invoked. There were mass arrests of government opponents and torture and deaths in detention. The NSMS was also responsible for internecine violence in black communities, engaging vigilantes and planting *agents provocateurs* to limit the influence of political groups there. The tricameral parliament established in 1983 was yet another constitutional instrument to co-opt the coloured and Asian people into the grand design of the regime. This led to the establishment of the United Democratic Front, which emerged during this period as the principal expression of resistance against apartheid.

It was amidst this enormous instability and repression that the church made its mark. Pastors were called on to minister to people and families brutalized by massacres and agitated by the military occupation which was a constant irritant in black communities. They felt the need to sharpen and focus the means to bring apartheid to an end. Whereas in the early 1970s the churches had some sympathy for the state, by the 1980s there was a deeper understanding of the liberation movements. Beyers Naudé, who became general secretary of the SACC, could confidently warn in 1983 that "unless new factors are going to play a role or unforeseen developments take place in the near future we will have to prepare ourselves for a long, protracted guerrilla struggle; a war increasingly fought with acts of sabotage and urban terrorism..."[7]

The SACC during the time of the general secretaryships of Desmond Tutu and Beyers Naudé saw the churches being engaged in fierce resistance against the state. This was resistance sparked by the Eloff Commission, which sought to control the foreign funding of SACC programmes. By the 1980s the churches were part of the resistance movement. Expressing this sentiment during a service in St George's Anglican Cathedral in Cape Town to protest detentions, Tutu underlined the theme of Christian resistance against unjust rule: "If we can no longer peacefully campaign for a change in an evil and unjust system, are the government saying then that the only alternative is violence — what else will be left for people to do?"

Tutu was overwhelmed by the international response of churches and ecumenical partners when he invited them to be present during the Eloff

Commission hearings as a token of solidarity for the church in South Africa, which was then on trial.

Beyers Naudé was general secretary when the WCC called the consultations in Harare (1985) and Lusaka (1987). In both instances the churches made valuable contacts with the leadership of the liberation movements. Both meetings issued strong calls for "comprehensive sanctions" with the support of the South African delegations. Lusaka, in addition, pronounced itself on the ethics of armed resistance to the system of apartheid. This statement was not rejected out of hand by South African member churches but was discussed at their synods during 1988.

The appointment of Frank Chikane as SACC general secretary in 1987 meant that the churches had entrusted someone with a reputation as a political activist with the task of leading the Christian conscience and action in resistance against apartheid. Chikane promptly refined the churches' solidarity work, especially in campaigning for sanctions against South Africa. He added his weight when he accompanied the Eminent Church Persons Group which visited Western governments engaged in substantial investment and trade relations with South Africa. In 1990 the SACC co-sponsored with the WCC a seminar on the illegitimacy of the South African government. Such actions were treasonable acts according to South African law, and it was uncertain that they would be supported by the SACC's member churches.

Chikane's leadership was one of enormous courage.[8] Having been one of the prime movers behind the Kairos document, he inspired the Standing for the Truth Campaign. He summarized his theological credo aptly when he stated that "the awakening of the social conscience and a knowledge of truth are central to evangelization, and are essential elements for church work and witness as a whole".

Thus, eventually, the South African churches responded to the challenge of the WCC in positive ways. They grew from frightened and embattled churches to churches which resisted apartheid strenuously and expressed their independence from the state in their calls to protest, support for sanctions and ever-closer co-operation with the WCC without the suspicion and animosity of earlier times. This changing climate made it possible for the WCC general secretary Emilio Castro to be received enthusiastically when he was able to visit South Africa in October 1991 and for the WCC's central committee to hold its January 1994 meeting in Johannesburg. The bonds of solidarity and affection between the South African churches and the WCC have grown stronger since 1970. So sincere has this mutual solidarity been that the 1991 Cape Town conference, under the theme "Challenges to the Church in a Post-Apartheid South Africa", could make this solemn commitment:

The church is called to celebrate, proclaim and embody the values of the kingdom of God. It must summon each new age to face the challenge of the gospel. It must at the same time share in the struggle for a social order that meets people's immediate needs — especially those of the poor and marginalized. To both, the churches of South Africa and their ecumenical partners elsewhere are invited to commit themselves afresh.[9]

NOTES

[1] Quoted in *Annual Survey of Race Relations*, Johannesburg, SAIRR, 1970, p.53.
[2] In an unpublished ms., dated 1980, tracing the development of SACC policies.
[3] Quoted by Zolile Mbali, *The Churches and Racism: A Black Perspective*, London, SCM, 1987, p.50.
[4] Quoted in *Annual Survey of Race Relations*, SAIRR, 1970.
[5] For an exposition of the terms "state theology" and "church theology", see *The Kairos Document*.
[6] Charles Villa-Vicencio, *Trapped in Apartheid: A Socio-Theological History of the English-Speaking Churches*, Cape Town, David Philip, 1988, p.115.
[7] Dom Helder Camara Lecture, "For the Sake of Freedom", Free University in Amsterdam, 1 June 1993, p.9.
[8] For a brief history of the SACC in the last 25 years see Bernard Spong and Cedric Mayson, *Come Celebrate*, SACC, 1993.
[9] *From Cottesloe to Cape Town: Challenges for the Churches in a Post-Apartheid South Africa*, WCC/PCR, 1991, p.101.

7

The Church and Violence

CHARLES VILLA-VICENCIO

There is a time coming, and it is not far off, when church buildings in the townships will no longer be used for religious services. They will be taken over as fortresses for storing arms and waging war. The only church that will survive is the church of the houses and the streets, where Christian people are gathering and living out their faith in solidarity with all who struggle against oppression.[1]

These words, spoken by a black South African preacher in 1984 at the height of the struggle against apartheid, contain a contextual ring that most armchair theologians will never understand. The tragedy is that violence continued, even after the process for electing a non-racial, non-sexist government by universal suffrage to replace the notorious apartheid regime was firmly in place.

Some suggested that the blame for the continuing violence should at least partly be attributed to those within the churches who supported the armed struggle against apartheid. Their argument was a simple one: Once the genie is out of the bottle, it is impossible to get it back inside. "Violence is violence is violence. Once the monster has been released it cannot be controlled," a church leader observed in the wake of a massacre that occurred prior to the elections.

The presiding bishop of the Methodist Church of Southern Africa, Stanley Mogoba, told people gathered at the opening service of the WCC central committee meeting in Johannesburg in January 1994 that "Christianity has compromised with war for too long". He stated that while the Programmme to Combat Racism had caused pain, hurt and fear for many who thrived on racism, it had at the same time brought hope to the victims of racism. "How significant and appropriate it would be," he continued, "if the last battle against war and armaments were to be launched in South Africa, the place where the war against racism has been won, or is at least in the process of being won."[2] Bishop Mogoba's observation places in sharp relief the need to ask again precisely when (or whether) armed struggle can be theologically justified. It is through this lens that a South African assessment of the PCR programme to provide humanitarian aid to liberation movements fighting the horrors of racism in Southern African needs to be made.

All but the most ideological opponents of the WCC would concede that support for disciplined revolutionary violence as a last resort is not the same as legitimizing the kind of political violence that threatens to undermine the democratic process. Continuing charges against the churches for having fomented violence — whatever the motive — nevertheless remind us that the debate on the legitimacy of armed struggle has not yet been fully dealt with. Categories of violence still need to be clarified and the spectre of injustice identified again as the relentless underlying cause that sparks revolutionary violence. Greed and the unwillingness to turn away from privilege earned at the expense of others need, in turn, to be exposed as the sustainer of endemic violence.

In the cauldron of conflict, unambiguous debate on violence, war and revolution is difficult to sustain. Many questions are left unanswered. Others are not asked. Some issues are strategically ignored. Others are simply not faced. Formal theological debate is by definition a "second act". It emerges in response to lessons learned and insights gained in the "primary" and most important act — which is to witness to Jesus Christ. This is essentially what SACC general secretary Frank Chikane was saying when he addressed a 1987 symposium on theology and violence at the University of Cape Town.[3] Chikane argued that theological debate is a luxury that people in South Africa's townships simply did not have. In this kind of situation, a person is compelled "either to run for one's life or fight back in self-defence". "Church theologians," he continued, "are talking about the morality of the use of violence in the war, instead of doing something to stop the war by tackling its causes." It is absurd to expect violated and oppressed people to engage in abstract debate on terms set by theologians and bureaucrats removed from the site of battle.

It is essentially a different kind of violence which today could threaten the fledgling South African democracy. A different political situation prevails. In this context the church needs to reassess its position on violence, addressing unanswered questions which emerged in the heat of battle, to ensure that it learns from the struggle of the oppressed and equips itself to face new challenges. This essay seeks to provide an annotated agenda for a "debate about a debate" — a debate on the legitimacy of armed revolution that shook the theological foundations of the church from the inception of the PCR in 1969 through to the termination of the armed struggle by the ANC and, later, by the PAC. The issues involved continue to present the church with concerns as potentially explosive as any it has been required to face in modern history.

The PCR debate

The milieu within which the PCR debate was born was intense. Martin Luther King Jr lay dead from an assassin's bullet. In South Africa, Nelson Mandela and the other Rivonia trialists had been condemned to life imprisonment. Civil rights legislation had been passed in the USA, and in South Africa apartheid was being intensified. The mood of the time was captured in the address of James Baldwin to the Uppsala assembly, speaking "as one of God's creatures whom the Christian church has most betrayed".[4]

Some within the churches (essentially the victims of apartheid) gave unqualified support to the WCC decision to provide financial support to liberation movements in southern Africa. Others argued that the provision of humanitarian aid to oppressed people who had resorted to arms was insufficient. They saw this as lacking in the kind of costly solidarity that the oppressed people of the region could legitimately expect from churches that had supported the war effort against Hitler three decades earlier. Still others feared that the support for the liberation movements signalled a radicalization and politicization of the church, which they could not support. The realities of colonial and post-colonial wars in Africa and elsewhere in the third world were cited as examples of what could happen in an escalated military conflict in South Africa. A new-found interest in pacifism began to emerge in some circles. The tragedy is that this interest was rarely translated into systematic non-violent programmes of action against a government committed to the maintenance of apartheid. As such, opposition in the churches to the PCR grants largely degenerated into a diatribe against the WCC and "terrorism". No organized attempt was made to dismantle apartheid in some other way. When economic sanctions were promoted as an alternative to armed struggle, this too was rejected by most critics of the PCR grants in South Africa.

Some of the organizations involved in the earlier attacks on the WCC enjoyed the financial backing of the South African government and of various agencies in the West. Recently a new round of similar attacks on the PCR and liberation theology has been generated.[5] These attacks are not addressed in this essay. A response to what obscures and obfuscates often generates more heat than clarity. In addressing the more serious debate on the PCR, I suggest that its essence can be clarified in five propositions:

a) The negative reaction of member churches and others to the PCR decision to fund liberation movements emphasizes the extent to which the theological agenda is set by church leaders and theologians essentially unaffected by racism. The WCC leadership made every effort to hear and respond to the voices of the oppressed themselves. However, the financial power and political influence of the dominant forces in church, state and academia were such that they were able to ensure that the debate was waged on *their* terms, answering *their* questions and addressing *their* constituencies, on the basis of *their* presuppositions.

b) The PCR grants witness to the fact that decisive action divides churches. It was the actual grants from the Special Fund rather than theological and ethical debate on racism that precipitated the conflict. The old adage that theology divides while service unites did not apply. So decisive was the action of the PCR that the broader *theological* debate on violence was virtually ignored by those who opposed the grants.

c) Violence is differently defined by different participants in the debate. The Kairos document makes the point:

> The state and the media have chosen to call violence what some people do in the townships as they struggle for their liberation, that is, throwing stones, burning cars and buildings and sometimes killing collaborators. But this excludes the structural, institutional and unrepentant violence of the state and especially the oppressive and naked violence of the police and army... Thus the phrase "violence in the townships" comes to mean what the young people are doing and not what the police are doing or what apartheid is doing to people.

To ignore the broader context within which revolutionary violence occurs is theologically irresponsible. Documents and records of the PCR debate identify the extent to which the structural and repressive violence of apartheid was exposed.[6] But reactions from member churches and in the public media to the grants to liberation movements were almost exclusively in relation to revolutionary violence — often without any attention to the context within which it emerged. The South African armed struggle was often defined in relation to manifestations of terrorism of the worst kind that had occurred in various other parts of the world, rather than in relation to the actual apartheid situation against which revolutionary violence was aimed.

d) The PCR debate as such was marred in many instances by a theology of evasion. This is partly because, as already suggested, the heat of battle does not allow for adequate debate on violence. At the same time the WCC allowed itself to be put on the defensive when critics (with assistance from the public media) focused discussion on "terrorist violence" (*sic*). It insisted that its support for the liberation movements was for humanitarian purposes only (rather than for the supply of weapons). This allowed the focus of public debate to be shifted away from the more important theological focus on liberation, on what constitutes appropriate means of struggle in oppressive situations and on whether armed struggle is ever a legitimate form of struggle. In brief, the debate on armed struggle became separated from its social context. As such it was isolated from the theologically important category of liberation.

e) The PCR debate exposed a disconcerting willingness by Christians to live with violence, reflective of the high tolerance of killing by the majority of the Christian churches. Implicit in aspects of the debate was a willingness simply to accept the political suffering of human beings as inevitable. This tolerance of suffering by those who do not themselves suffer contributes to a milieu within which revolution is often seen by the oppressed people as the only alternative to oppression.

A theological agenda

The importance of *theology in the face of battle* lies in the poignancy of the questions raised. The challenge of *theology as a second act* is to employ these questions as a basis for rethinking the teaching of the church on the issues involved. In what follows, an attempt is made to propose an agenda for doing so.

Discernment

A key ingredient of the PCR's South African involvement was the search for a prophetic, analytical understanding of the ambiguities of a political process that sustained racism, economic exploitation and human deprivation. The WCC doggedly committed itself to an analysis of black suffering in South Africa. In so doing, it bolstered the international campaign for economic sanctions (described by Donna Katzin in Chapter 4) and other non-violent measures designed to undermine apartheid. The arms industry, the violation of the oil embargo and the collaboration of certain multinational companies with the apartheid regime were repeatedly brought under the spotlight of critical enquiry by the WCC. The Council's willingness to act on its insights gave the church a credibility among the poor that few can question or doubt. At the height of the PCR controversy, Zambian President Kenneth Kaunda observed: "The WCC's visionary action... may well be seen in the future as decisive for the church's fate in southern Africa."[7]

In moving beyond neutrality; in "taking sides" through providing material support for organizations committed to armed struggle, the WCC located risk at the centre of its theological agenda. Churches threatened to withdraw from the WCC, and some actually terminated their membership. Others suspended or curtailed funding of the WCC. The refusal of WCC leaders to capitulate to these pressures, while continuing to give material expression to their analytical insights and theological convictions, constitutes a reality of contemporary church history that deserves a focused study of its own. It bears witness to the kind of prophetic ministry on which the church dare not renege.

The theological issues involved in the armed conflict of the 1970s and 1980s remain pertinent to consideration of the manifestations of violence in society today. The lines of battle are less clear now than they were earlier. The ambiguities of struggle have intensified. Violence has become endemic. Factions are seeking to undermine the democratic process in South Africa. Fears exist that "little will change" for the average South African. These factors make analytical discernment more urgent than ever before. Questions abound: How can the violence be stopped? Who is behind it? Whose interests are being served as the cycle of violence continues? What kind of response to structural, political and criminal acts of violence can be regarded as theologically legitimate? To many such questions there are no simple answers. Context, motives and ultimate goals are decisive ethical categories. Debate around these issues within a nation-building context has scarcely begun.

Ecumenical monitoring is necessary to ensure that historic compromise between black and white nationalisms does not degenerate into a deal between a white elite and a black middle class that only perpetuates an economic system which inevitably leaves the marginalized and poor of the land sidelined and alienated. A nation divided against itself in the wake of generations of the divide-and-rule policies of apartheid is likely to have to defend itself against rogue elements and non-democratic forces within its own ranks. Attention will need to be given to questions about what constitutes the legitimate use of force to prevent the total collapse of the nation.

A theology that fails to scratch where it hurts most will ultimately fail to be prophetically effective. A theology which stubbornly fails to promote the cause of the poor surrenders its biblical mandate. At the same time, the question posed in the WCC study on *Violence, Non-violence and the Struggle for Social Justice* is a pressing one: how can former oppressors (and their families and friends, who may themselves have been victims of violence) be integrated "into the liberated society... we are fighting for?" To fail to address this concern could have serious consequences for the future.

St Thomas Aquinas observed that "an error about the world redounds in error about God".[8] Leonardo and Clodovis Boff insist that, while the prime object of theology is God, theologians before asking what oppression means in God's eyes must ask the more basic question about the actual socio-political and economic nature of oppression and its causes.[9]

Central to the continuing debate on violence is an ability to discern and understand the nature of the violence, the purposes of the violence and the long-term effects of violence of whatever kind on the social fabric. Prophetic witness is absolutely dependent on this continuing analysis. Any attempt to provide an appropriate theological critique of violence without the most rigorous forms of social analysis constitutes little more than a form of theological self-indulgence, incapable of making any lasting impact on the stubborn realities of the time.

The PCR engaged in a programme of rigorous social analysis in the 1970s and 1980s to eradicate apartheid. The new challenge involves radical discernment, designed to ensure that the emerging new society ultimately serves the needs of the poor. This theological need to defend and promote the interests of the poor is a priority which the church needs to continue to affirm.

Violence

When if ever is violence theologically justified? Responding to concerns about the funding of liberation movements (expressed primarily by churches in the USA and Europe, supported by white Christians in South Africa), the WCC repeatedly pointed out that the funds were for humanitarian aid, not arms. The WCC further emphasized that this aid came from a Special Fund designated for this purpose, not from general funds the WCC received as membership fees and other donations.

Jan Love's response to this emphasis, made in an address to the Cape Town conference during the October 1991 visit of WCC general secretary Emilio Castro, is important:

> This explanation... begs the question that our detractors know so well: the WCC and PCR deliberately took a high-profile stand in solidarity with movements that used violence. Whether or not they use money for weapons, these movements still engaged in armed conflict. Indeed, some part of our constituency argued on occasion that we should take a further step in joining arms with them. Clearly the WCC and the PCR have not chosen this route. [10]

The majority of Christian churches and organizations — including the WCC, SACC and SACBC — are not pacifist. Guided by a just war theology (and in some circles by talk of just revolution), these churches and ecclesial bodies have at the same time been haunted by pacifist teaching. Just war theory was intended to limit war, to prevent Christians from drifting into the other "Christian" positions on violence, namely holy war or crusade theology. To use a just war argument self-righteously to justify the killing of others is a violation of New Testament teaching. At the same time, just war theory is a doctrine grounded in a realism which suggests that killing may in certain circumstances be necessary — for a *just cause* (above all as an act of self-defence), in pursuit of a *just end*, using *just means*, as a *last resort*, by a *legitimate authority*.

The PCR decision to fund liberation movements in South Africa did more than all the text books on the subject had ever done to focus the minds of some Christians in South Africa — not least those bearing the brunt of apartheid oppression — on the theological implications of war. Seeking to keep alive the pacifist challenge of the early church within this debate, Sigqibo Dwane argues that a qualitative shift has taken place in theological thinking: "Once the step of accepting and justifying violence under certain circumstances had been taken, however special these circumstances, the church lost its pristine innocence. Christian identity could never be the same again."[11] Malusi Mpumlwana describes what is involved:

> The theological problem facing the church is how to hold the challenge of the early church and the need to compromise on the use of violence in creative tension. The logic goes something like this: The Christian church is fundamentally pacifist, but under certain circumstances there may and probably should be consideration for the use of violence to prevent a greater evil. From a theological-ethical perspective, the pertinent question is whether it is possible to establish viable criteria against which to measure any deviation from the norm of pacifism.[12]

Debate on the interpretation of the criteria for justifiable war — and indeed on the just war theory itself — continues.

The decision of the PCR to provide humanitarian support for liberation movements that had resorted to armed struggle in South Africa was based on a fundamental belief in the legitimacy of the liberation cause. In terms of the "creative tension" described by Mpumlwana, the PCR grants were made at the nexus of "just cause" and "ambiguous means" — realizing that the resort to arms invariably brings additional suffering to oppressed and innocent people even if it eventually attains its goal of liberating the oppressed.

At the same time, nonviolent response to oppressive violence evokes similarly ambiguous consequences. The PCR grants gave expression to a strand within ecumenical social thought which showed "a growing reluctance to condemn categorically those groups which feel obliged to use force in attacking entrenched social, racial and economic injustice".[13] Committed "to clarify (not to terminate) the churches' debate",[14] the WCC passed no judgement on those who resorted to violence as a means of securing their liberation. It recognized that in some situations "choices about the use of force and violence... cannot be avoided".[15]

While the severest criticism of the WCC came from member churches who opposed the Special Fund grants, some within the member churches criticized the WCC from a different perspective. They argued that once it was concluded that the resort to violence by the oppressed people could not be theologically condemned, the possibility of Christians taking up arms in solidarity with those who opted for war could not be excluded. Clearly a decision by the WCC to fund arms purchases would have split the ecumenical movement. More important is the question whether this should be seen as the task of the church. The advocacy, interpretation and moral discernment which the church can render in situations of conflict may well be a service more important than the supply of arms.

When forces opposed to the liberation struggle realized that the theological ideas behind the distinction between humanitarian aid and money for guns would be lost in public debate, they quickly seized the opportunity to shift the focus of debate away from questions of liberation *per se*. Broader questions concerning oppressive structures, within which oppressed people "find themselves already in situations of violence in which they cannot help but participate", were ignored. [16] The outcome was a high-profile public debate on armed rebellion and revolution, isolated from a debate on institutional violence and oppression and ignoring the theological and political right of people to be free.

All forms of violence were not treated in an even-handed manner. The extent of the violence against marginalized and abused people in numerous situations around the world — whether blacks, women, the aged or the young — was simply not adequately addressed. It seems that the fundamental concern of the most vociferous critics of the WCC grants was not, in fact, primarily the issue of violence. To what extent did racial and economic factors influence the response of some opponents of the PCR grants who simply refused to allow that apartheid was so evil as to warrant armed rebellion?

At the same time, the focus on humanitarian aid evoked concerns of a different kind, allowing the impression that the church was backing off from the ultimate consequences of its own theology. The criticism of the Kairos document of what it calls "church theology" is that the church all too often seeks to stand above the fray, offering ethical comment. Clearly the WCC did take sides in South Africa. The public debate that followed, however, was such that most member churches were able to take refuge in discussions of the ethical correctness of a particular strategy. In so doing, they left other options which they could have employed as non-violent strategies against apartheid largely unexplored. The obvious exception to this was the call for economic sanctions, and in South Africa at least this option met with as much opposition as did the decision to provide humanitarian aid for liberation movements fighting the regime.[17]

The Lusaka meeting (1987) went further than any other ecumenical statement on the question of violence:

> While remaining committed to peaceful change, we recognize that the nature of the South African regime which wages war against its own inhabitants and neighbours compels the liberation movements to use force along with other means to end oppression. We call upon the churches and the international community to seek ways to give this affirmation practical effect in the struggle for liberation in the region and to strengthen their contacts with the liberation movements.[18]

Some of those most deeply engaged in the struggle against apartheid hoped Lusaka would provide a stronger statement, and feelings ran high during the debate. Most of the white church leaders in South Africa felt the Lusaka statement had gone too far, and it came to symbolize the deep division the liberation struggle had produced within the church in South Africa. After hostile and antagonistic debate, the Lusaka statement was adopted by the SACC national conference, with most blacks voting for its adoption and most whites opposing the resolution.

To have expected a fragile ecumenical movement divided against itself to have gone further than it did in the Lusaka statement is unreasonable. But "second-act" theology must now face the questions that could not be adequately addressed earlier. The question is whether, with the pathos of the moment of struggle over, the church can muster the motivation to do so.

Non-pacifist churches must give a more decisive answer to the question of precisely what violence can be theologically justified and under what circumstances. Above all, they need to face the bias of just war theory in favour of the existing order — under the guise of "legitimate authority". This requires giving theological consideration to the nature of legitimate rule and government, which might be the most important theological contribution the churches can make to the democratic process — the most effective antidote to tyranny and, ultimately, revolution. If the biblical message is indeed about liberation, rebellion by the poor and oppressed ought to be responded to theologically with more understanding than the institutional and repressive violence of the oppressor. Recognizing that just war theory constitutes a compromise position in relation to the example of Jesus and the witness of the early church, it is the church's responsibility to devise an ethic that orders society in such a manner that the "inevitable compromise" of war and revolution is a rare and last resort. At the same time, the church must continually be asking about the nature of its responsibility in a just war situation.

Non-violence

Cases of theological support for crusades, state violence, war, massacres, executions and tortures are legion. In South Africa the history of church complicity in violence includes a missionary enterprise linked to the military conquest, a theological justification of colonial and apartheid domination and a willingness (through uniformed chaplains and a refusal to support conscientious objection) to identify with an oppressive army. The readiness of most Christians (whether in support of institutionalized or revolutionary violence) to accept a priori that violent behaviour is a necessary part of society is left largely unchallenged by the majority of WCC member churches.

Visiting Mozambique in 1987, Desmond Tutu observed: "International action and international pressure are among the few non-violent actions left. Yet how strident is the opposition to economic sanctions... If this option is denied us, what then is left? If sanctions should fail, there is no other way but to fight."[19] When individual groups have sought to find non-violent options for change — and there are examples of this stretching back to the earliest days of colonization — the support they need for such actions has not been forthcoming from all the Christians within the ecumenical movement. Ironically, when a group of South African Christians announced in 1985 that because the institutional churches were opposed to armed struggle and to economic sanctions as ways of ending apartheid, they would call for prayers to end the unjust rule, this too was opposed by many prominent white church leaders in the country![20]

That the churches have not applied themselves to non-violent options for social change with the same dedication as the liberation movements have shown in the struggle against apartheid is a case of failing to take seriously their own theology of humanity created in the image of God. This doctrine means that the abuse and destruction of human life violate God's creation — while non-pacifists argue that in certain circumstances transgression of this norm may be condoned in order to serve the greater good of humanity. It also means that the God-given endowment of humanity with creative powers will come to expression in rebellion and revolution when avenues for realizing these gifts are denied. Where a system of government denies people their right to realize their full humanity and express themselves through democratic participation in government, resistance is ultimately inevitable. In the absence of all other options, it is perhaps the only act that can give adequate expression to what it means to be human.

This dimension of the irresistible will and unquestionable right of people to be free, grounded in a biblical understanding of creation, did not come to full expression in the public debate on the PCR grants. It is this which gives such importance to the decision of the WCC central committee at its meeting in Johannesburg in January 1994 "to confront and overcome the spirit, logic and practice of war and to develop new theological approaches which start not with war and move to peace, but with the need for justice".

Non-pacifists and pacifists alike have an obligation to create a cultural, socio-economic and political order which includes sufficient space for the realization of human creativity. To deny this space constitutes a form of structural violence which can only result in rebellion. The report of the Corrymeela consultation on the study of violence and non-violence gives expression to this reality, which was suppressed under the public outcry against "terrorism".

> In many situations the church has been effective in a pastoral (or chaplaincy) role to the victims of violence and oppresssion. Its capacity as a prophetic institution needs to be developed. It needs to become more discerning in perceiving the roots of violence, more far-sighted in recognizing factors leading a society towards violence and more courageous in exposing these factors, thus taking a lead in the struggle. This will confront the church with the dilemma of opting, at least in the short term, for disturbance against stability. This will lead along the uncertain, risky, ambiguous way of the cross. The actual lead will most likely come from prophetic individuals. The church as well as society has tended to murder the prophets; but it is they who will enable the church to become a prophetic sign for humanity. [21]

Ministry

The PCR grants to liberation movements placed the challenge of ministry in a new perspective. On the basis of what the WCC called (at the time) "brotherly solidarity" with oppressed people who resorted to arms, the grants gave tangible expression to this solidarity. South African member churches were, generally speaking, critical of this stance. [22] A resolution adopted by the Methodist Church accusing the WCC of political partisanship and calling for the end of "unconditional grants" captured the sentiments of most white non-Methodist Christians as well. [23] In response WCC member churches in South Africa established Justice and Reconciliation committees committed to finding alternative ways of addressing racial and other divisions within the churches. Some specifically committed themselves to finding ways of ministering to those "on the other side" — the words used by the churches at the time.

The history of this endeavour, together with the debate surrounding uniformed chaplains in the South African security forces, is well documented in *War and Conscience in South Africa: The Churches and Conscientious Objection.*[24] Churches whose membership includes people fighting on different sides of the border (a situation every one of the WCC member churches in South Africa faced) were confronted with the challenge of how to provide effective ministry to revolutionary forces. In failing to respond adequately to this challenge, the church was seen by many to be on the side of the existing order. Despite resolutions and declarations to the contrary, this is what their pastoral practice suggested. The challenge of ministry in conflictual situations must remain high on the agenda of the church.

The PCR lesson

For those who are not pacifists, no less than for those who are, the challenge is to continue to search for non-violent ways of bringing about social justice across barriers of race, economics and what may well prove in South Africa to be even more impenetrable — sex. Women continue, in most cases, to be excluded from the decision-making structures of society, while statistics show that the abuse of women is on the increase. It is estimated that in 1990 one woman of every six in Cape Town was the victim of domestic violence.[25]

Political and criminal violence also characterize South African society. In 1990 the Institute of Contextual Theology published a document on *Violence: The New Kairos*, discerning a pattern of violence which suggested the involvement of a "third force". "There is a fox behind the wolves who are killing us," a Soweto woman is quoted as saying.[26] The document is more pertinent today than when it was first published. It would be foolhardy for the ecumenical movement to think that the kinds of issues raised in the PCR debate are now a thing of the past. It would be a tragedy if the lessons learned since the founding of the PCR in 1969 were considered as no more than past history.

The new challenge facing PCR, as encapsulated in the resolution of the WCC central committee meeting in Johannesburg, provides a new opportunity to redress the historic imbalances of apartheid and eradicate the violence which threatens the very existence of the South African nation as presently constituted. The issues involved are often less clear than was the case in fighting the all too obvious horrors of apartheid. This requires a level of motivation and commitment from the churches greater than anything that went into the earlier PCR strategy devised to eradicate apartheid. It remains to be seen whether the churches have the spiritual resources and moral vision required to meet the challenge.

NOTES

1 Quoted by Margaret Nash, "Ecumenical Vision and Reality in South Africa", in Charles Villa-Vicencio & John W. de Gruchy, eds, *Resistance and Hope: South African Essays in Honour of Beyers Naudé*, Cape Town, David Philip, and Grand Rapids, Eerdmans, 1985, p.148.
2 This has been suggested, inter alia, by John Kane Berman, executive director of the South African Institute of Race Relations, SAIRR press release, 4 February 1993.
3 Frank Chikane, "Where the Debate Ends", in Charles Villa-Vicencio, ed., *Theology and Violence: The South African Debate*, Johannesburg, Skotaville, 1987, p.302.
4 *The Uppsala Report*, p.130.
5 Cf. Rachel Tingle, *Revolution and Reconciliation*, London, Christian Studies Centre, 1992; Joseph Harris, "The Gospel According to Marx", *Reader's Digest*, February 1993, pp.33-38.
6 See the statement by the WCC central committee, "Violence, Nonviolence and Civil Conflict", 1973, pp.22-24; also the report of the Corrymeela consultation, "Violence, Nonviolence and Civil Conflict", 1983. Both published in *Violence, Nonviolence and Civil Conflict*, Geneva, WCC, 1983.
7 Kenneth Kaunda, *On Violence*, London, Collins, 1980, p.121.
8 Quoted in Leonardo & Clodovis Boff, *Introducing Liberation Theology*, Tunbridge Wells, UK, Burns & Oates, 1987, p.25.
9 *Ibid.*
10 Jan Love, "The WCC and the Struggle for Racial Justice in Southern Africa: Past, Present and Future", in *From Cottesloe to Cape Town: Challenges for the Church in a Post-Apartheid South Africa*, WCC/PCR, 1991, p.85.
11 Sigqibo Dwane, "Early Christians and the Problem of War", in Villa-Vicencio, ed., *Theology and Violence*, p.144.
12 Mpumlwana, "War, Violence and Revolution", in Villa-Vicencio & J.W. de Gruchy, eds, *Theology and Praxis*, Vol. 2, *Ethics in a South African Context*, Cape Town, David Philip, 1994.
13 *Violence, Nonviolence and Civil Conflict*, p.11.
14 *Ibid.*, p.5.
15 *Ibid.*, p.21.
16 *Ibid.*, p.28.
17 See Charles Villa-Vicencio, *Trapped in Apartheid: A Socio-Theological History of the English-Speaking Churches*, Maryknoll, NY, Orbis, and Cape Town, David Philip, 1988, pp.117-24.
18 *The Church's Search for Justice and Peace in Southern Africa*, Report on Meeting in Lusaka, 1987, Geneva, WCC, 1987, pp.28-29.
19 Desmond Tutu, "Freedom Fighters or Terrorists?", in Villa-Vicencio, ed., *Theology and Violence*, p.77.
20 Allan Boesak & Charles Villa-Vicencio, eds, *When Prayer Makes News*, Philadelphia, Westminster, 1986.
21 *Violence, Nonviolence and Civil Conflict*, p.14.
22 The response of the various South African member churches to the PCR programme is detailed in Charles Villa-Vicencio, *Trapped in Apartheid*.
23 *Ibid.*, pp.113-14.
24 London, Catholic Institute for International Relations and Pax Christi, 1982.
25 See Jane de Sousa, *Behind Closed Doors*, Cape Town, Catholic Welfare and Development, 1991, p.15.
26 *Violence: The New Kairos*, Johannesburg, Institute of Contextual Theology, 1990, p.7. See also Thomas Cochrane, *Behind the Violence in South Africa*, Braamfontein, Christian Citizenship Department, Methodist Church of Southern Africa, 1992.

8

The Task Ahead

PHILIP POTTER

"Let us join hands and march together into the future... We have reached the end of an era." So spoke Nelson Mandela, who on 10 May 1994 became the first democratically elected president of South Africa. Thirty years earlier, when he was on trial for treason, he had declared:

> I have cherished the ideal of a democratic and free society in which all persons live together in harmony and with equal opportunities. It is an ideal which I hope to live for and to achieve. But if need be, it is an ideal for which I am prepared to die.

Now, after a long struggle in which many have died and in which Mandela and others like him have had "no easy walk to freedom", he reiterated that commitment before the vast international assembly gathered to greet his inauguration.

Mandela's personal integrity, magnanimity towards his former opponents and prophetic vision of justice and peace for all the peoples of South Africa shine like a rainbow of hope over a storm-clouded world. But he knows that the struggle to turn that vision into material reality will continue to be a long one. He inherits a land fraught with social and economic problems and still suffering from the aftermath of a violent history. It remains a major task of the churches and of the ecumenical movement across the world to continue to help South Africa to create the conditions that will advance the well-being of its peoples and establish a society of justice for all and a lasting peace.

A culture of violence

It must be remembered that South Africa was the first place in Africa south of the Sahara in which Europeans really settled. That was in 1652, just four years after the end of the Thirty Years War in Europe, during which over 40 percent of the population perished and untold destruction was wrought. A group of some fifty settlers accompanied Jan van

Riebeeck, the agent of the powerful Dutch East Indies Company, and arrived in the Cape. By 1680 more than 600 Dutch were living in Cape Town. Soon after the revocation of the Edict of Nantes in 1685, there arrived 300 Huguenots who had been expelled from France. Other Europeans, mainly Germans, followed.

Their contact with the indigenous people was violent from the start, and this violence marked the history of the relationship. Land was taken by force, communities were destroyed and people were subjected to becoming segregated servants. Slaves were brought in from East Africa, Indonesia and Malaysia, and later indentured labourers from China and India. The coming of the British — first in 1795, more permanently in 1806 — brought new elements of violence — between the European peoples and against the blacks, as the whites moved eastwards and northwards. The blacks were never docile. They resisted forcefully, but the superior arms of the whites were their undoing.

In the nineteenth century, commerce, agriculture and farming brought South Africa into the world capitalist economy. The discovery and mining of diamonds and of gold led to the pass laws and the segregation of blacks under armed control. The struggle between the Boers and the British was fierce and bloody, especially during the war of 1899-1902. However, the blacks paid the heaviest price in life and status. The Zulu rebellion of 1906-1908 was ruthlessly put down.

After the British established the Union of South Africa in 1910, the way was set for enacting the Natives Land Act. This later ensured that 87.3 percent of the land would be in the hands of whites, leaving the blacks the much less arable 12.7 percent. The process of making the blacks a dispossessed servant class, without rights, and forcibly confined to a small space in urban and rural areas, went on steadily and relentlessly, until from 1948 the Afrikaner National Party created a fully racist, apartheid police state with a panoply of restrictive legislation. This system was unique in the world, as was the capitalism founded on racial exclusion and oppression. South African society was grounded on and has been maintained by violence for over three hundred years.

It is therefore understandable that in the process of changing from a police state to what F.W. de Klerk called in his historic speech on 2 February 1990 "a totally new and just constitutional dispensation", violence exploded in the black townships and areas. The conditions of life in the townships are lamentable — poor housing, inadequate social, health and educational facilities, conflicts between long-time residents and those released from prison back from exile, broken homes, drunkenness, drugs and crime. Matters have been further complicated by old ethnic rivalries and conflicting interests. Underlying all this is the rage about the long years of oppression and segregation. It has been said that people become like those whom they oppose. This was all the more evident in South Africa because of the brutalizing and dehumanizing activities of the police, security forces and vigilantes in the townships and rural areas.

A shared humanity

It was in this situation of violence that Christians and other activists sought to work and witness for a more peaceful environment. One of the remarkable realities is that the majority of blacks (including coloured and Asians) have never given in to oppression. They have found all sorts of ways of surviving and maintaining some community life. They have a traditional word for this — *ubuntu*, shared humanity. This is particularly true of the leadership given by women. There are community-based groups, funded by various non-governmental organizations (NGOs), operating in the cramped and dilapidated townships and other such residential areas. There is an active Education for Democracy campaign, which helped to prepare people for voting in the elections and for participating in local decision-making and action.

One significant ecumenical activity, sponsored by the South African Council of Churches, the South Africa Catholic Bishops' Conference and the WCC, is the Ecumenical Monitoring Programme in South Africa (EMPSA), which has been operating since September 1992, monitoring violence in several townships and also helping the electoral process in close collaboration with local churches, other faith communities and civic bodies. It will continue to work for some time to come to promote a more peaceful atmosphere.

The WCC central committee, at its meeting in Johannesburg in January 1994, agreed to "establish a programme to overcome violence". It declared:

> The purpose of this programme is to challenge and transform the global culture of violence into a culture of just peace... There is need to confront and overcome the spirit, logic and practice of war and to develop new theological approaches consonant with the teachings of Christ, which start not with war and move to peace, but with the need for justice.

It is in this spirit of justice for the poor and the oppressed that the WCC and its member churches must urgently appeal to the international community and the new government of South Africa to make a significant gesture now in favour of the black community by providing substantial funds to meet the crisis situation in the townships and elsewhere. This should help to facilitate job creation and training, better housing, health care and education for the neediest as quickly as possible. It would be a clear sign of the promise of change to a more just and caring society, and help to lessen the prevailing violence. Such action would require intensive, ongoing and constructive co-operation between the state, international bodies, trade unions, management and the wider NGO community.

Similarly, some clear gesture must be made in favour of the rural people who have long been deprived of arable or grazing land and thus have little or no possibility to earn a living. Considerable thinking on the crucial land problem has already been done in South Africa itself by church and community groups. What is being proposed is a crash programme in favour of the neediest as the prelude to a fully worked out and costed plan of land reform throughout the country. As a matter of urgency, churches have an obligation to conduct a public survey of their own disused arable land and consider making this available to those communities in greatest need.

A caring economy

Beyond these emergency measures, the pressing task for the WCC and its member churches is to give particular attention to the economic situation of South Africa. The country's economic structures and wealth have been inextricably bound up with the racist and apartheid system. In no other country in the world has almost 80 percent of the population been so excluded from participating freely and normally in economic life except in subordinate and restricted positions.

Though the media and angry church people attacked the WCC for showing solidarity with the liberation movements through humanitarian grants, the main thrust of the PCR was to expose the racist economy of South Africa and the connivance of multi-nationals, banks, foreign industries and others in maintaining the racist system and profiting handsomely from it at the expense of the blacks. The most important action of the WCC was to call for the withdrawal of investments, loans and industrial enterprises from South Africa and for comprehensive sanctions. In the end, it was the determined resistance of black people and the economic and financial repercussions of international sanctions which brought about the decision of the government under F.W. de Klerk to initiate a change of the system. But what radical change will the new government be enabled to make?

In his address to parliament in February 1990, De Klerk had a carefully worded section on the economy. Here are some sentences from it:

> A new South Africa is possible only if it is bolstered by a sound and growing economy, with particular emphasis on the creation of employment...

The central message is that South Africa too will have to make certain structural changes to its economy, just as its major trading partners had to do a decade or so ago...

The government's basic point of departure is to reduce the role of the public sector in the economy and to give the private sector maximum opportunity for optimal performance. In this process, preference has to be given to allowing the market forces and a sound competitive structure to bring about the necessary adjustments.

By means of restricting capital expenditure in parastatal institutions, privatization, deregulation and by curtailing government expenditure, substantial progress has been made already in reducing the role of the authorities in the economy.

These sentences are clearly in line with the present stage of global capitalist thinking and practice. They are also the language of the International Monetary Fund and the World Bank — especially such words as privatization, deregulation and "curtailing government expenditure". In most cases these code words mean that in order to become competitive, severe cuts must be made in education, health and social services and increased unemployment occurs.

Following this section on the economy, De Klerk went on:

...Poverty, unemployment, housing shortages, inadequate education and training, illiteracy, health needs and numerous other problems still stand in the way of progress and prosperity and an improved quality of life... The conservation of the physical and human environment is of cardinal importance to the quality of our existence.

What is intriguing is that hardly any linkage is made between these two sections. How will the decreasing role of the government in the economy help to meet the urgent socio-economic and environmental problems?

In the 1993 Human Development Report of the UN Development Programme there is a chapter on "People's Participation", which is defined thus: "Participation means that people are closely involved in the economic, social, cultural and political processes that affect their lives." It goes on to say that "large numbers of people continue to be excluded from the benefits of development". It specifically points out that in South Africa the blacks have been a marginalized majority, and quotes the following facts:

In a country where the richest 5 percent of the population, mostly white, own 88 percent of all the private property, half the population, mainly black, live below the poverty line. The lives of over half of poor black children are being stunted by malnutrition. A third of the black population over 15 years of age are illiterate. Three-quarters of black teachers are either unqualified or underqualified for their job. The education system thus perpetuates a vicious circle of deprivation and discrimination. For South African blacks the achievement of full political rights would be a vital step towards greater participation. But unravelling apartheid completely will be a complex and difficult task in the years ahead.

The UN Development Programme puts the emphasis on "the achievements of full political rights", but does not address its own description of the appalling economic and social conditions under which the black people continue to live. The demands made by the present free market competitive economy, especially by the International Monetary Fund and the World Bank, do not go in the direction of meeting the needs of the marginalized black community. Unless definite decisions are made to meet the unique situation in South Africa, the rich and the protected white people will continue to enjoy the wealth at the expense of the oppressed poor. This would result, in the new situation, in utter chaos. That is why articulating a biblically based position concerning a viable economy for a just and responsible society is critically important for the WCC and the SACC and their member churches.

At its inauguration in 1948 (the very year when the apartheid state was formally established in South Africa), the WCC set forth the criteria for judging political and economic systems as follows (readers must excuse the sexist language of those days):

> Man is created and called to be a free being, responsible to God and his neighbour. Any tendencies in state and society depriving man of the possibility of acting responsibly are a denial of God's intention for man and his work of salvation. A responsible society is one where freedom is the freedom of men who acknowledge responsibility for justice and order, and where those who hold political authority or economic power are responsible for its exercise to God and the people whose welfare is affected by it.
>
> Man must never be made a mere means for political or economic ends. Man is not made for the state but the state for man. Man is not made for production, but production for man. For a society to be responsible under modern conditions it is required that the people have freedom to control, to criticize and to change their governments, that power be made responsible by law and tradition and be distributed as widely as possible through the whole community. It is required that economic justice and equality of opportunity be established for all members of society.

The statement made by the SACC in September 1993 on "The Church and Ethical Investment in South Africa" outlines the Code of Conduct suggested for businesses operating in South Africa (see Appendix 1). It quotes the statement from an ecumenical conference held in February 1992 which tries to give a Christian perspective on economics and the questions which should be answered in relation to it:

We understand that economics is neither an end in itself nor does it represent an autonomous sphere with natural laws of its own. We hold that economic activity has to be judged on the basis of the extent to which it provides for all people, particularly for the poor, the marginalized and the oppressed. In that context we ask:
— Does economic activity enhance life?
— Does it promote social justice?
— Does it encourage democracy and participation?
— Does it preserve the integrity of creation?

The economy is a worldwide concern, evoking a clear test of our biblical faith, and addressing it is probably the most pressing ecumenical task in the years ahead. An SACC/WCC consultation in 1991 called for "a caring economy".

A crucial church

South Africa is economically the most powerful state in Africa, and particularly in relation to its neighbours. In recent years it has played a dominant and destabilizing role in the countries surrounding it. The WCC and the All-Africa Conference of Churches are aware of these wider relationships and the need to mobilize the churches to joint action. A WCC consultation on "Peace, Democracy and Violence", held at Windhoek, Namibia, in December 1993, agreed to an overall goal to "enhance and increase the capacity of the churches and the peoples of Africa in playing a useful role towards a just, peaceful, participatory and sustainable society" and in particular "to promote national, regional and pan-African cooperation in the search for peace and sustainable development".

In South Africa the churches and Christian organizations have a crucial role to play. *The Kairos Document: Challenge to the Churches* (1985 and 1986) made a critique of "state theology" and "church theology". Quoting the preamble of the constitution of the Republic of South Africa, which identified the state and the history of the Afrikaners with that of Israel, it noted that the white Dutch Reformed churches had subscribed to this idolatrous and heretical theology of identifying Almighty God with their history and present life. But the Kairos document went on to make a critique of church theology, referring mainly to the English-speaking churches. This is a theology which regarded the apartheid state as legitimate; which made judgements on the political situation from the vantage point of the privileged and not from that of the oppressed and poor; and which retreated at critical moments into spiritual counsel only.

The reason the Kairos document and its exhortations have so much force is that South Africa's population is 77 percent Christian — almost a miracle, considering the long oppression of black people by those who invoked the Scriptures to justify their inhuman actions. It is evident that many Christians were enabled, one way or another, to discover for themselves the God of the oppressed who sustained them in their struggle. But many of these Christians regarded the institutionalized churches as obstacles to the struggle for justice and human dignity. There is also the undoubted fact that many white Christians found their way to identify with the cause of black people and have been willing to face the consequences of their stand.

Nevertheless, recent research on the situation of the younger generation in South Africa (between 16 and 30), has produced surprising data. It indicates that 56 percent of the women and 37 percent of the men in this age group attend a worship service once a week. But only 12 percent of the young people are actively involved in political organizations. It is difficult to know whether this represents the poverty of the churches in helping young people to be politically engaged for positive changes in society, or whether they have little confidence in political organizations. This is serious, because all political organizations will have to rethink their role in South Africa. This applies especially to the ANC and other political groups which will have to change from strategies of resistance to those of building up the life of the nation for the well-being of all.

A keen observer of and participant in the South African scene has emphasized that the church has a tremendous task in affirming respect for all human life and the whole of God's creation. This should lead people to accept one another, to have respect even for the enemy and the life of a criminal and to be prepared to forgive. The important theological issue here is that while a new national constitution can provide for basic human rights and for the pursuit of justice for all people, it is the churches which can help young people and all citizens to discern that these rights are derived from our biblical faith.

While the Kairos document has rightly been recognized as a prophetic tract of our times, little has been made of the Rustenburg declaration, which emerged from the fully representative national conference of South African church leaders in November 1990 on the theme "Towards a United Christian Witness in a Changing South Africa". The WCC and some of its member churches were represented at this meeting. The conference's clear statement was: "On this we are all agreed: the unequivocal rejection of apartheid as sin." In an act of confession, as representatives of the churches in South Africa and throughout the world, they said:

> We confess our own sin and acknowledge our heretical part in the policy of apartheid which has led to such extreme suffering for so many of our land.

We denounce apartheid in its intention, its implementation and its consequences as an evil policy. The practice and defence of apartheid as though it
were biblically and theologically legitimated was an act of disobedience to
God, a denial of the gospel of Jesus Christ and a sin against our unity in the
Holy Spirit.

It is important to reflect on the three major kinds of guilt expressed:

> Some of us actively misused the Bible to justify apartheid, leading many to
> believe that it had the sanction of God. Later we insisted that its motives were
> good even though its effects were evil. Our slowness to denounce apartheid as
> sin encouraged the government to retain it.
>
> Some of us ignored apartheid's evil, spiritualizing the gospel by preaching
> the sufficiency of individual salvation without social transformation. We
> adopted an allegedly neutral stance which in fact resulted in complicity with
> apartheid. We were often silent when our sisters and brothers were suffering
> persecution.
>
> Some of us were bold in condemning apartheid but timid in resisting it.
> Some churches failed to give effective support to courageous individuals at the
> forefront of the protest against evil. We spoke out for justice but our own
> church structures continued to oppress. We blamed other churches and were
> blind to our own inconsistencies.
>
> In our desire to preserve the church we have sometimes ceased to be the
> church... We have continued to move in separate worlds while claiming to be
> one Body... Most of all, we have been unwilling to suffer, loving our comfort
> more than God's justice and clinging to our privilege rather than binding
> ourselves to the poor and oppressed of our land.

Confession was followed by affirmative statements calling for "acts of
restitution in the fields of health care, psychological healing, education,
housing, employment, economic infrastructure and especially land own-
ership. For many years greed has led to the taking of land from the poor
and weak. Both church and state must address the issue of restoring land
to dispossessed people."

Unfortunately, there has been little effective follow-up of all the brave
statements made at Rustenburg, nor has there been a serious effort to
consider their implications for a wider ecumenical fellowship than at
present exists in the SACC. But it remains as a clear expression of the
tasks facing the churches of South Africa and all the member churches of
the WCC.

A continuing vigilance

The point which has been made again and again in the writings of
South Africans is that so little of the fundamental teaching of the Bible in
relation to our time and context gets through to the congregations and in
the day-to-day witness of Christians. Charles Villa-Vicencio's recent

book of interviews entitled *Spirit of Hope* includes the testimonies of many leading South African personalities, in all walks of life, who found their inspiration for the struggle for racial and social justice in the Bible or in their religious tradition. Alas, they also experienced the poverty of the church in proclaiming and living out the message.

In 1994 the SACC organized an inter-church conference called Vision '94. Its theme was "The earth is the Lord's and everything in it" (Psalm 24:1). A "Proclamation to the Christians of Southern Africa" said: "We must assist in devising ethically driven, people-centred economic structures primarily concerned with the eradication of poverty, disease and ignorance...; we must monitor and promote the ethical code of investment and economic policies, believing that the needs of people, including work, are basic human rights." The conference pledged "that all the people of God should take initiatives to form ecumenical clusters in ministering to our extended local communities". They made a commitment "to continued vigilance reasserting the prophetic role to ensure justice in society by working for a strong and active church in civil society". Here was a determined effort to get Christians from the grassroots to make their own what had been said in meetings of Christian leaders. It was a call to renewal of the whole people of God for witness and service in association with people of other faiths and all people of good will.

South Africans are determined to move from a theology of resistance to a theology and action of reconstruction. This is a task which the member churches of the WCC are called to take up in fellowship with their brothers and sisters in South Africa. Experience has shown that the WCC and its member churches do not find it easy to move quickly from a prophetic stance to acts of witness and service. We have not been sufficiently vigilant in recognizing the continuing task after the main struggle against racism. The case of South Africa has been the most difficult and persistent because so many interests have been involved. The process of change to a non-racial, non-sexist, democratic society working for the common good will be stubbornly long and arduous.

During the past twenty-five years of struggle, many member churches of the WCC have had difficulties about taking a clear stand on South Africa. Their countries and in some cases they themselves had much invested in the racist state. It was in the awareness of this failure of the world Christian fellowship that the WCC assembly at Canberra in 1991 aligned itself with the confession made by the South African churches in the following words:

> We join in the spirit of the National Conference of Church Leaders in South Africa which gathered in Rustenburg, in confessing before God and one

another the ways in which we have permitted, supported and refused to resist the dehumanizing, oppressive system of apartheid. To the extent we have allowed our sisters and brothers to suffer humiliation, dispossession and death for so long under this oppressive system, we have denied the gospel of Jesus Christ and violated our unity in the Holy Spirit.

How will this confession be turned into acts of bringing forth fruits worthy of repentance? The ecumenical community maintained the call for sanctions against the apartheid regime until it was satisfied that real changes towards democratic structures were taking place. Several churches have been involved in the Ecumenical Monitoring Programme in South Africa and also in giving many kinds of material and other aid. However, a democratic constitution in South Africa will not necessarily bring about actions towards justice for the oppressed poor. Much will depend on real, costly decisions by the industrialized nations and international financial institutions. This means that the churches and action groups will have to keep themselves well informed, highly organized and aggressively active. They need to continue pressing these governments and institutions to change their economic and financial relations with South Africa in a way which will enable the new government to give priority to the clamant needs of those who have for so long been excluded from enjoying a reasonably human existence.

The WCC central committee meeting in Johannesburg in January 1994 called on the churches of South Africa "to seize the opportunity to construct a new, inclusive and vital ecumenical movement to confront the challenge to reconstruct and reconcile South Africa" (see Appendix 2). This is also a call to the WCC itself and its member churches to seize this opportunity to become prophetic witnesses in word and deed in confronting the challenge of South Africa, which is a microcosm of the challenge posed all over the world.

We are not sufficient in doing these things. But Christ is sufficient — he who has sustained the millions who have suffered and died and yet witnessed in faith, hope and love. May the WCC and all the churches therefore dedicate themselves anew to the tasks ahead "in the power of Christ's resurrection and in the fellowship of his sufferings" (Philippians 3:10).

It seems appropriate to end this record of a long struggle and the task ahead with an old Zulu saying: "When a thorn gets into the toe, the whole body stoops to pick it out."

Code of Conduct for Business Operating in South Africa

SACC Initiative, July 1993

Introduction

The apartheid system has historically burdened South Africa with gross economic distortions, stagnation, secrecy, severe discrimination and natural devastation. It has deprived the country's workers, communities and environment of the fundamental rights written into international conventions and upheld in other countries.

In order to reverse this crippling legacy and to improve the economic well-being of all South Africans, investment by both South African and multi-national companies needs to be reshaped in the image of an equitable, democratic and life-enhancing society.

It is out of this grave concern and motivation based on ethical religious considerations that the South African Council of Churches, meeting in conference on 8 July 1993, takes this initiative to introduce and support this code of conduct. The code outlines ways in which business can play a constructive and creative role in partnership with workers, communities and other members of civil society, to lay the economic foundations for a stable and prosperous South Africa.

While these standards are also expected to inform the policies of a democratically elected government, in the interim, they are designed to apply to companies operating in South Africa.

1. Equal opportunity

Companies should ensure that their operations are free from discrimination based on race, sex, religion, political opinion or physical handicap, and implement affirmative action programmes designed to protect the equal rights and treatment of the historically disadvantaged.

2. Training and education

Companies should develop and implement training and education programmes to increase the productive capacities of their South African employees in consultation with the trade union movement.

3. Workers rights

Companies should recognize representative unions and uphold their employees' rights to organize openly, bargain collectively, picket peacefully and strike without intimidation or harassment.

4. Working and living conditions

Companies should maintain a safe and healthy work environment and strive to ensure that the working and living conditions they provide accord with relevant international conventions.

5. Job creation and security

Companies should strive to maintain productive employment opportunities and create new jobs for South Africans.

6. Community relations

Companies should share information about their practices and projected plans with communities affected by their operations, and develop social responsibility programmes in ongoing consultation with representative bodies in these communities.

7. Consumer protection

Companies should inform consumers of any possible dangers associated with their products and cooperate with consumer protection and broader community organizations to develop and uphold appropriate product safety and quality standards.

8. Environmental projection

Companies should utilize environmentally sound practices and technologies, disclose how and in what amounts they dispose of their waste products and seek to minimize hazardous waste.

9. Empowerment of black businesses

Companies should strive to improve the development of black-owned South African businesses by purchasing from and sub-contracting to such firms.

10. Implementation

Companies should cooperate with monitors established to implement these standards by disclosing relevant information in a timely fashion.

APPENDIX 2

Statement on South Africa

Adopted by the Central Committee of the WCC
Johannesburg, 20-28 January 1994

South Africans are a singing people. We have not sung because we were happy. We have sung even when we cried. We have sung so as not to allow ourselves to be broken. We have sung to survive.*

The central committee of the World Council of Churches, meeting for the first time in South Africa, gives thanks to God that the light of hope has been kept burning among the people of this land through the deep dark night of apartheid. We thank God that we have been able, at long last, to join with our Christian sisters and brothers here together in new songs of praise and thanksgiving, at the dawning of a new day.

Our hosts from the churches joined in the South African Council of Churches have said "thank you" through us to Christians and churches in the most distant parts of the world. Thank you for having been constant in prayer for, and in solidarity with, the people of South Africa through decades of pain and struggle.

On behalf of the oikoumene, we say "thank you" many times over to our South African sisters and brothers. Thank you for teaching us to sing in a new way; for your example of unity when forces on all sides seek to divide; for your faith; for hope shared in hours of deep despair; for your young people who, across many generations, galvanized the country to change. We thank you especially for the theological clarity you have provided to the whole church, which illuminated the truth that racism is a sin which is deeply rooted in the structures of nearly every society and that its theological justification is a heresy; for helping us to acknowledge our own complicity when our churches remained silent about the heresy of apartheid and the racism in our own countries, and when we acquiesced in the support many governments and businesses gave the apartheid regime.

---

* From the opening worship at the WCC central committee meeting in Johannesburg, South Africa, 20 January 1994.

South Africa today abounds in new hope, bought with the blood of martyrs. The names of some ring out wherever people struggle for justice throughout the world. Others we will never know by name, yet we are humbled and honoured by their sacrifice.

Today, former mortal enemies are seeking to construct a new, unified, non-racial society together. A revolution of momentous proportions is being achieved through skilful, innovative, peaceful negotiations all around the country, laying the foundations for a new, democratic South Africa.

However miraculous, such sweeping change does not yet constitute justice. The deep-seated economic and social problems created by apartheid's multi-layered, highly structured system of exploitation, oppression and social fragmentation are even more resistant to change than the formal political structures. So, transformation is plagued by growing poverty, unemployment, social dislocation and homelessness. Judging from the experience of other African nations seeking to make the transition to democracy, the poor could be hurt even more by the practices and policies of institutions which administer the international financial and trade system. As it is, change comes far too slowly for the worst victims, especially for the youth and women, who are particular targets of violence, even within the apparent security of their own homes. They all fear that change will never reach all the way to them. Frustration and anger grow, breeding revolt and acts of revenge.

At the other end of the spectrum, threats to the privileges of those who benefited from apartheid breed fear and hatred.

These contradictions, escalating crime and lawlessness, and politically motivated violence in Natal and the East Rand all pose present dangers. They put great pressures on those negotiating for peaceful change. It is true that political violence has claimed a terrible toll in human life since 1990. But South Africa is not in a state of civil war, contrary to the impression often given both at home and abroad.

Terrible as it is, violence is only part of the present reality. South Africa is a land bubbling with new ideas and constructive initiatives arising from local levels. New ministries of reconciliation are being formed every day. Many people are being trained in methods of mediation and conflict resolution. Many people are monitoring violence. Free legal assistance groups are being created. Forums comprising a variety of organizations of civil society were created to work out proposals on particular aspects of the interim constitution as a contribution to building a non-racial, non-sexist South Africa. Local economic and social initiatives are building up community and providing skills training.

Education for democracy programmes are at work and voter education workshops are being held around the country. Very many of these are the initiative of youth and of women, who are especially effective and well-organized. Gradually, a new culture of peace is taking shape to replace the culture of war and violence.

The recent experience of many other societies which were consumed by violent passions stemming from ancient, unresolved enmities before they could complete hopeful transitions to democracy shows that this shift of culture is essential. Through negotiation, enemies can find an alternative to conflict, but if its achievements are to be lasting, it must move on to reconciliation through the painful process of confession, repentance, forgiveness and compromise. This is an integral part of the reconstruction of society.

Changes in the global political environment provided a catalyst for the process of liberation from apartheid. A healthy, peaceful and just global and regional context will remain essential as South Africa transits into the future. It has been fully integrated into the global economy for most of this century, and heavily dependent on foreign investments. Some see in the present change, with the relaxation of international economic and other sanctions it has allowed, an opportunity to reintegrate the South African economy into the "first world". But South Africa cannot ignore its immediate South African context. In a document on "Contemporary Challenges to Africa" which we are commending to the churches we have explored that context more fully.

Recommendations

In light of these facts, and deeply committed to the future of South Africa, the central committee of the World Council of Churches, meeting in Johannesburg, 20-28 January 1994:

1) affirms the right of all citizens of South Africa to participate in the forthcoming elections and urges that the necessary provisions be made;

2) appeals to those parties in South Africa who remain outside the framework of negotiation to risk moving forward together, to trust the good intentions of the negotiators and, by joining them, to make their own contributions to this process which offers the only present hope for peace and justice for all;

3) urges governments and international financial investment and trade institutions to support the Transitional Executive Council and the parliament soon to be elected in their efforts to reconstruct society through the total reform of national structures of governance, and of the national economy, including the elimination of corruption;

4) urges governments to recognize that a strong civil society is essential to good governance and participatory democracy, and for this reason not to abandon their support for the non-governmental organizations which contributed greatly to change, and are now key instruments for the rebuilding of community at the most basic level of society;

5) urges those now preparing the transformation of South Africa, and those who will be given major new responsibility for governing this nation, to commit themselves to ensuring women their rightful place of leadership at all levels and in all sectors of society;

6) urges the United Nations, other governments and international non-governmental organizations, including the churches, to respond to the invitation of the Transitional Executive Council and non-governmental bodies like the South African Council of Churches to send and help train sufficient monitors to ensure free and fair elections unhampered by violence on 27 April 1994;

7) appeals to the member churches of the World Council of Churches not to slacken in their prayers, moral or financial support for the South African Council of Churches and its member churches in this time when ecumenical witness presents new opportunities and challenges in which people look to their churches for leadership;

8) appeals to the international community and to the churches to recognize the heavy cost paid by the frontline states and neighbouring countries like Lesotho, Swaziland and Botswana, and to assist them in their recovery from the consequences of apartheid so that the hope for a new day may be realized throughout southern Africa;

9) urges especially support for the present efforts of the churches of South Africa in education for democracy and voter education;

10) calls upon the South African government at all levels, business, churches and other non-governmental organizations to strengthen the hand of the youth of South Africa through:
   — the provision of equal educational opportunities at all levels, including compulsory primary and secondary education;
   — the establishment of clear goals for the eradication of illiteracy;
   — the strict implementation of child labour laws corresponding to international standards;
   — the elaboration of emergency youth employment schemes;
   — ensuring that youth are full participants in decisions which will shape the South Africa they will inherit; and
   — encouraging young peoples' innovative approaches to community building and reconciliation;

11) calls upon all the churches of South Africa:
   — to assume their full responsibility for peace, reconciliation, unity and reconstruction of the society;
   — to recognize and give effective support to the women's organized efforts to create a violence-free society and to ensure within their own structures the values of a non-sexist society;
   — to persist in the search for a new moral community based on values and norms which recognize and promote the value of the human person, of community and of family in order that all may contribute to society; and
   — to seize the opportunity to construct a new, inclusive and vital ecumenical movement to confront the challenge to reconstruct and reconcile South Africa;

12) calls on Christians and churches here and around the world to be constant in prayer for persons who have been placed in responsible positions to oversee the period of transition, to prepare the forthcoming elections, and for those who will be elected to office, that they perform their functions in such a way as to cause future generations to honour them as the mothers and fathers of the new South Africa.